THE NATIONAL TRUST BOOK OF
PICNICS

Jackie Gurney

DAVID & CHARLES
Newton Abbot   London   North Pomfret (Vt)

QUANTITIES AND CONVERSIONS

In all the following recipes the approximate metric equivalents have been given in brackets after the imperial measure, eg 1 lb (450 g) plain flour. Although not exact—1 lb in fact equals 453.6 g—these equivalents are accurate enough for practical cookery purposes, as grams and millilitres are so small that plus or minus five makes very little difference.

The metric abbreviations used are: g = gram; kg = kilogram; ml = millilitre. A teaspoon is equivalent in metric terms to 5 ml; a tablespoon to 15 ml.

For American readers: 1 tbsp = 1½ US tbsp; 2 tbsp = 3 US tbsp; 1 pt = 2½ US cups; 1 dessertspoon = about 1 US tbsp. The Imperial pint is 20 fl oz whereas the US pint is 16 fl oz.

British Library Cataloguing in Publication Data

Gurney, Jackie
   The National Trust book of picnics.
   1. Outdoor cookery   2. Picnicking
   I. Title
   641.5'78   TX823

   ISBN 0-7153-8099-0

Typeset by ABM Typographics Limited, Hull
and printed in Great Britain
by Redwood Burn Limited, Trowbridge, Wilts
for David & Charles (Publishers) Limited
Brunel House   Newton Abbot   Devon

Published in the United States of America
by David & Charles Inc
North Pomfret   Vermont 05053   USA

CONTENTS

ACKNOWLEDGEMENTS

I do not pretend that all the recipes are my own invention. Some are, of course; others are old favourites, and I have included what I consider to be the best version for outdoor eating. Help of every conceivable kind came from friends and relatives, in particular: Sally Varlow, Jan Watts, Roy Cornwell and the English Country Cheese Council, Dr Martin Park, Lady Olga Maitland, Janet Rolls, Lady Bagge, Lisbet Mason, George and Sally Fuller, Katharine Garner, Shirley Coates, Rosemary Joekes, June Gapp; and not forgetting members of my family who never want to hear the word 'picnic' again. For specialist advice I turned to the Flour Advisory Bureau, British Farm Produce Council, British Duck Advisory Bureau and Alcan. To them all, many thanks, and especially to Warren Davis, whose idea it all was in the first place.

INTRODUCTION

What is it about picnics? Why are they so popular? And why is it that the British in particular hold them so dear?

I have asked myself these questions time and time again in the course of writing this book. I do not believe that we are a particularly hardy race, nor, necessarily, are we lovers of the great, wild outdoors. Mad dogs and Englishmen may go out in the midday sun when abroad, but the latter almost certainly prefer the comforts of a garden deckchair and shady porch when at home.

Is it then the untamed savage lurking beneath the British breast that drives us out to seek wild adventures and isolated romantic retreats? Hardly, given our traditional abhorrence of self-expression. Is it our response to the high cost of our restaurant food, as one disgruntled visitor put it: 'There stands an Inn below the hill, rightly named 'Pelican' from its enormous bill.' Perhaps it is a combination of all these things; perhaps it is just the natural reaction of a heavily populated, heavily industrialised society that wants to take a 'breather' whenever the opportunity presents itself.

What is certain is that some people take their picnics very seriously indeed. No time or expense is spared acquiring the nattiest primus, the coolest cool-box or one of those new-fangled coffee pumps that saves you the trouble of taking the top off the thermos.

It would be nice to think that the same degree of enthusiasm goes into the choice of picnic food—but this is rarely the case. How often do you see a picnic spread that is truly mouth-watering, prettily set out and garnished, and with carefully chosen drinks served at the right temperature? Picnics should be light-hearted, fun-packed things and as interesting to prepare as they are to eat. Forget the 'Mother-knows-best' type of foods; aim instead for something a little more imaginative—and memorable. Take heart from the thought that food tastes better in the open air and in congenial company, so if you do make a ghastly mistake it is unlikely that anyone will notice it.

The following is a collection of recipes that will provide food for thought—and, I hope, just a little amusement—for a variety of different picnics. I have chosen recipes that are not too taxing (assuming you wish to emerge fresh and lively from your kitchen); that do not involve a trek to Harrods to buy the ingredients (the exception is grouse); and that provide healthy portions for outdoor appetites.

THE HISTORY OF PICNICS

The origin of the word 'picnic' is shrouded in mystery. The *Dictionary of English Etymology* states that Lord Chesterfield first introduced it to our language in 1748. He was writing to his son and used the word quite casually as though it was a term of common usage. Yet 'picnic' did not find its way into the English dictionary until many years later.

In France, the word *piquenique* was recorded by Ménage in 1692 and said then to be of recent introduction. In Germany, *picquenic* was the term for an eighteenth-century Hanoverian ball. In Italy and Sweden, etymologists have traced usage of similar words back to various forms of social entertainment. Georgina Battiscombe, who wrote a most erudite study of English picnics, published in 1949 by Harvill, claimed that though the history of the word seemed to point to a French origin, its only possible etymology suggests that the roots are English. 'Of the derivation of the word, or who was its inventor,' she writes, 'we profess ourselves ignorant.'

'Picnic' has also changed in meaning over the years. Originally it was a contributor feast, to which each member of the party brought along a share of the food and drink. 'A picnic supper', says *The Times* of 18 March 1802, 'consists of a variety of dishes. The subscribers to the entertainment have the bill of fare presented to them with a number against each dish. The lot which he draws obliges him to furnish the dish marked against it, which he either takes with him in his carriage or sends by a servant.'

It is unlikely that these early picnics were held out of doors. Nor did their popularity lie in their economy as do the contributor bottle parties of today. Perhaps it was the gastronomic one-upmanship that was so appealing, or perhaps it was nothing more than a diversion, a novelty entertainment for a section of society with too little to do and too much time to do it in.

No sooner had the word 'picnic' been introduced than it became notorious. The Picnic Club was formed early in the century as a 'harmless and inoffensive society of persons of fashion'. Its members included George IV, when Prince of Wales, and Mrs Fitzherbert, his mistress. Although their occasion consisted chiefly of a theatrical event followed by a picnic supper, public opinion declared the proceedings improper. As a result the club gained a bad reputation, and that of the picnic was similarly besmirched.

From thenceforward, 'picnic' became associated with things trifling and inadequate. 'Picknickery and Nicknackery' was a popular nineteenth century way of saying what would pass as unimportant, inconsequential, or even 'what a load of rubbish' in the twentieth. Around this time Gillray produced a savage caricature called 'The Picnic Orchestra', depicting leading society ladies, Lady Salisbury and Lady Buckinghamshire, attempting to be musical. The Picnic Club might have existed for only one year (1802–3) but it had a long-lasting effect on its namesake, transforming its meaning from a run-of-the-mill social event to a light-hearted, fashionable and almost risqué frolic.

The additional meaning of picnic as an outdoor party with a repast, the definition we accept today, must have come about not long after the Picnic Club's demise. In *Emma*, published in 1817, Jane Austen writes of a proposed excursion to Box Hill and mentions a picnic in connection with it. Alas, poor Emma's 'quiet, unpretending, elegant' outing is turned into a 'regular eating and drinking and picnic parade', thanks to the intervention of the awful Mrs Elton and the amiable bumbler, Mr Weston. Only the social cross-fire of the conversation saves the event from being one of the most unsuccessful picnics on record!

Although the association of outdoor eating and the picnic is not yet two hundred years old, records of meals taken outside go back centuries. In those days *al fresco* eating was not necessarily organised with pleasure in mind. In the majority of cases, travellers wending their weary way over rough roads and dirt tracks would have had to take their provisions with them and eat out in all weathers, taking whatever shelter they could. What appears to be the first 'picnic' on record is to be found in the 'Chronicle of Reginald, a monk of Durham'. He describes the arduous journey of the monks of Lindisfarne who, in the last half of the ninth century, left their island monastery under threat of Danish invasion and carried the sacred relics of Saint Cuthbert to a new resting place on the mainland. For food, the monks were forced to rely on the charity of the country they were passing through, but since it was a time of famine these provisions were few. 'Even the head of a horse was scarcely able to be bought for ten pennies of silver,' records Reginald, writing three hundred years later.

Not all travellers fared as dismally as the monks of Lindisfarne. Chaucer's pilgrims enjoy plenty of feasting and carousing, but they were relatively wealthy, and the route to Canterbury was plentifully supplied with hospitable inns. Not for them the uncertainties and discomforts of outdoor eating.

Much early travelling must have involved make-shift catering, and in the days of a peripatetic monarch and court, hundreds if not thousands of mouths would have to be fed. At Longleat in Wiltshire,

7

the stately home of the Marquess of Bath, it is said that Queen Elizabeth I decide to 'drop in' to see the house during her western progress of 1575. Unfortunately for the owner and builder of Longleat, Sir John Thynne, the house itself was not complete, so her Majesty had to be suitably entertained by what must have amounted to a massive picnic in the grounds outside.

A popular form of outdoor feasting in Tudor and Stuart times was the hunting picnic. In the British Museum there is a splendid account of an Elizabethen hunting picnic; George Turbevile's *The Noble Arte of Venerie*. In it the hunt begins and ends with a picnic, which is described in verse, while the fare provided is as mouth-watering today as no doubt it was then:

> For whiles cold loins of veal, cold Capon, Beef and Goose With pigeon pies, and mutton cold, are set on hunger loose, And make the forlorn hope, in doubt to scape full hard, Then come and give a charge in flank, else all the rest were marred, First neats' [ox] tongues powdered well, then gambones [gammon] of the hog, Then sausages and savoury knacks, to set mens' minds on gog.

Accompanying the verse is an illustration showing Queen Elizabeth I sitting down to the feast, with a tidy cloth spread before her, and courtiers in various stages of serving food, pouring wine and generally making merry. The prodigious quantities of wine and ale in the picture are linked to an old superstition that unless the huntsman drinks long and hard before the deer carcase is broken up, the venison would putrify.

Picnicking purely for pleasure, as opposed to that occasioned by travelling or hunting, was then, as now, chiefly a summertime occupation. May was the most popular month for pleasure picnics, and how welcome it must have been after the cold winter months spent in dark, draughty houses without our modern comforts of central heating and electric lighting! The celebration of May Day and outdoor festivities during this month of lovers goes back to the Middle Ages; and children then, as now, go gathering 'Nuts' (a corruption of knots, meaning bouquets) of the flowering May.

By the eighteenth century, form and fashion had decreed the end of such informal parties, at least in polite society. This was the age of entertainment in the grand manner, of elegant town and country houses designed for lavish hospitality. The creation of elaborate gardens, fashionable in Europe in the seventeenth and eighteenth centuries, provoked a new passion for outdoor eating, which had long been a feature of Mediterranean life. In Italy in particular, it had reached a peak of perfection. Travellers on their Grand Tour were fascinated by the pavilions, grottos and arbours, some furnished with stone or marble tables and chairs. Everything was done to combine the comforts of indoors with the enchantment of outdoors.

Following this example, gazebos, follies, and domed pavilions sprang up like mushrooms in the extensive parks of the landed gentry. Many examples still survive in the care of the National Trust—the temples, Pantheon and shell-lined grottos at Stourhead in Wiltshire; the fully equipped banqueting house, the Ionic Temple, at the Rievaulx Terrace in North Yorkshire; the superbly elegant Temple of the Winds at Mount Stewart in Northern Ireland; and the more mysterious castle at Saltram in Devon. The three latter examples were equipped with subterranean kitchens where 'invisible' chefs were purported to have conjured up meals as if from thin air.

Elaborate water parties were conceived with gilded barges propelled by liveried boatmen, accompanied by the inevitable barge full of musicians. On one such occasion in 1715, George I and his royal party, voyaging from Whitehall to Limehouse, were entertained by a set of short pieces written specially for the journey. The King was so entranced, he bestowed a special pension on the composer—and so Handel's Water Music was born.

With the advent of the nineteenth century, the word 'picnic' caught on, and thereafter its popularity was not to be hindered. The Romantic Movement, typified by the Rousseau nature cult, was beginning to hold sway in Britain. By Victoria's reign, one response to it was expressed in a sudden liking for the more rugged beauties of our native land, by impromptu outings often accompanied by sketchbooks and watercolours, or by whimsical expeditions to archaeological ruins.

Queen Victoria in the Highlands—a luncheon at Cairn Lochan, 1861 *(The Mansell Collection)*

9

The Bear's Hut, Killerton House, Devon *(Severn-Smith Photographic)*

The classical temples and Mediterranean-style pavilions were replaced first by chalets, then by rustic huts of thatch and bark—romantic notions of the poor workingman's cottage. At Killerton House in Devon, owned by the National Trust, a splendid example of such a hut is still preserved. The Bear's Hut has always been a favourite with children and in the 1890s it was kept ready and stocked with apparatus for nursery tea—faggots in the fireplace and crockery in the cupboard.

The most passionate romantic of all the Victorians must surely have been the Queen herself. Brought up in a stiflingly formal environment, Victoria could scarcely have known what it was like to live as a normal person, enjoying privacy and family life, away from prying eyes. Until, that is, she and Prince Albert discovered Balmoral where the formality of their existence was tempered by expeditions into the hills, by shooting, sketching, and, naturally enough, by picnics.

The form of Victoria's picnics is recorded faithfully in *Leaves from the Journal of our Life in the Highlands*, the Queen's own work. The routine varied but little: Albert would devote himself to field sports or improving the estate, while she would chase after him on her little pony led by the indispensable John Brown. A lunch spot would be settled on, often the 'little housie' or bothy that Albert had had built at Feithort, and the lunch partaken with the minimum of comfort.

The Victorian love affair with outdoor life, combined with the expansion of the British Empire and the greater freedom to travel brought by the railways, resulted in an upsurge of social activity. The weekend out of town was just beginning, heralding a new kind of country-house pleasure party. People generally, and women in particular, were becoming more active, indulging in sports such as lawn tennis, croquet, walking, cycling, hunting and shooting. Picnics became an essential part of that enjoyment, especially as the desire to explore spilled overseas.

The ingenuity of the British in taking their customs and pleasures abroad knew no bounds. Miss Emily Eden, sister of Lord Auckland, Governor-General of India, recalls a picnic breakfast she enjoyed whilst visiting him: 'Our breakfast was laid out in a sort of side-aisle of grotesque Hindu columns, and at each column was a servant with a long stick keeping off the monkeys from the tea and chocolate.' On other expeditions of a wilder nature, monkeys were probably among the least of the worries to confront the intrepid picnicker.

The turn of the century and the Edwardian period saw what was probably the apogee of picnics in the grand manner. In *The Edwardians* J. B. Priestley talks of 'processions of food and drink from eight in the morning until late at night'. Certainly the Edwardian picnic was no exception. Edward Spencer in *Cakes and Ale* writes of hampers laden with game pie, pressed beef, boar's head, foie gras, devilled larks, stuffed quails, and plovers' eggs served on a bed of aspic. The champagne and brandy flowed like water while all around the servants stood like statues, patiently awaiting the completion of such Bacchanalian revelry, so that they could clear up the empty dishes and return to their household chores.

Yet, if the scale of our appetites has decreased along with our pockets, our appreciation of the picnic is surely undiminished in the latter part of this century. Certainly the contents differ greatly—strange little packets of dehydrated meats and vegetables instead of bulky stores on expeditions; and the barbecue now makes an appearance at even the most impromptu gatherings. The equipment we use to transport food to the picnic site—insulated picnic boxes, thermos flasks and plastic containers—must surely make the job of organising a picnic so simple compared to the lengths to which our forebears went. And of course we have the motor car, that blessing and blight of the modern age, that takes us out into the wilds and, hopefully, gets us back again.

11

FAMILY PICNICS

It only takes a glimmer of weak and watery British sunshine to bring picnicking families into the open. On any warm weekend or bank holiday you will see them out in force on the highways and byways; or, in the case of a city such as London, gathered like wasps around the jampot on any available patch of greenery.

Even in those cramped conditions there is something akin to escapism in a picnic. You are shutting the family door on unpaid bills and unmown grass; you are gathering together to face the uncertainties of journey, of weather, of destination. There is expectation and excitement in the air. You are once again the noble savage living the simple life as God and Jean Jacques Rousseau intended—or at least you would be if only the person nearby would turn off his radio.

These days there is yet another avenue for picnic escapism. Barbecues, imported from our cousins across the water, are now the essential ingredient of any successful summer party. Perhaps we are sublimely optimistic—and terribly British—in our devotion to this new found toy despite the disasters it can bring. We cling to it through many a downpour, only pausing to wonder as we nibble our half-cooked, mostly-charred offerings if this is what living in America is really like. The answer, of course, is that a good barbecue demands American-style efficiency to set it up. The rest is usually plain sailing, despite the British climate; it is the preliminaries that are essential.

Once you have mastered the art of barbecueing successfully then you will want to do it again and again, for nothing can equal the mouth-watering smell and delicious smoky, crusty taste of food cooked over charcoal. Surely that is why family barbecues, as part of picnics, have become so immensely popular with every level of society from the Queen downwards. The Royal family always picnic during their annual summer holidays at Balmoral. The food and provisions are packed into baskets and taken in the back of a Land-Rover to their favourite lakeside site. Here the Duke of Edinburgh takes charge of the cooking—usually sausages and chops—while the Queen makes the salad. The salad dressing is her acknowledged speciality!

To hold a successful picnic or barbecue in this climate you need to be an opportunist. It is no good anticipating the event several weeks in advance—as like as not when the day dawns it will be pouring with rain. Family picnics must therefore be 'get up and go' affairs.

12

A picnic at Netley Abbey, Hampshire, in 1883 *(The Mansell Collection)*

The picnic basket itself can be anything from the glamorous fully fitted wicker variety from somewhere like Harrods costing as much as five hundred pounds, to a battered old suitcase or even a cardboard box. As well as the usual picnicking gear (plates, all-purpose carving knife, bottle opener etc) ice boxes, or 'coolies' as the Australians call them, are also essential. It is a good idea to chill them before putting in food or drink by pouring in some cold water with a handful of ice cubes and letting the box stand for half an hour or so. Then, just before you are about to set off, empty out the water and pack the base of the box with plastic bags full of ice, or with two or three of the plastic freeze bricks (or bags) that can be bought from ironmongers or hardware shops. This will keep your picnic fare icy cold for at least a couple of hours. If you plan to take a barbecue with you then a further store of equipment is required: matches, firelighter, charcoal, long-handled barbecue tools, tongs for handling the coals, etc.

The National Trust and many privately owned historic houses also welcome picnickers, at least on some parts of their properties. You would be hard-pressed to find a more beautiful spot to set out your picnic spread than in the park-like meadows of Killerton House, Devon, or on the sunny south lawn of the walled garden at Felbrigg Hall, Norfolk. All they ask in return, in addition to a modest entry fee in most cases, is that you parcel up all your litter and dispose of it properly in the bins provided, or even better, take it home. Surely this is a small price to pay for the privilege of eating in such beautiful surroundings.

Summer Vegetable Soup *(serves 6–8)*

2 baby turnips, sliced
4 oz (125 g) carrots, sliced
4 oz (125 g) new potatoes, scraped
    and sliced
6 young leeks, sliced
2 sticks celery, sliced
Few French or runner beans,
    sliced

Handful of fresh peas
1 oz (25 g) butter or dripping
2 rashers streaky bacon,
    derinded and chopped
3 pt (1.75 l) stock or hot water
Salt and freshly ground black
    pepper
Grated cheese to garnish

Prepare all the vegetables and cook them gently in a large saucepan with the fat and bacon for about 15 minutes. The saucepan should be covered and shaken from time to time to prevent sticking. Add the stock and seasoning, bring to the boil and simmer gently until all the vegetables are tender (about 45 minutes).

Sieve or liquidise the soup in small amounts: reheat and pour into a large thermos flask or jug. Serve with the grated cheese.

Stuffed Cornettos *(serves 6 as a starter, 3 as a main course)*

4 oz (125 g) cucumber
3 oz (75 g) button mushrooms
1 stick tender celery
4 oz (125 g) cream cheese
1 tablespoon mayonnaise

Paprika
6 thin slices Mortadella sausage
Lettuce leaves and gherkins to
    garnish

Dice the cucumber and mushrooms finely. Sprinkle with salt and leave for 1 hour. Slice the celery finely.

Mix the cream cheese and mayonnaise together in a bowl. Season with paprika and combine with the cucumber, mushrooms and celery. Put a spoonful of the mixture on each of the sausage slices, spread it over the whole surface and roll up. Wrap the cornettos tightly in foil. Chill in the refrigerator for a couple of hours before packing into the picnic hamper. Serve garnished with lettuce leaves and gherkins.

Tunny Fish Dish *(serves 6)*

1 oz (25 g) butter
1 tablespoon cooking oil
1 medium onion, peeled and finely
    chopped
1 cup long-grain rice
2½ cups chicken stock
1 lb (450 g) carrots

3 eggs, hard-boiled
1 x 7 oz (200 g) can tuna fish
Salt and freshly ground black
    pepper
¼ pt (150 ml) mayonnaise
Handful of salted peanuts and
    fresh parsley to garnish

Melt the butter and oil in a heavy saucepan and gently cook the onion for about 5 minutes or until soft. Add the rice and stir so that the grains are well coated. Add the chicken stock and bring to the boil, stirring once or twice. Reduce the heat to simmer and cook gently for 10–15 minutes or until tender. Meanwhile, peel and dice the carrots and cook them until soft in salted boiling water. Hard boil the eggs and slice in half when cool. Open the tin of tuna fish, remove any skin and bone, and flake the fish in a mixing bowl.

Allow the rice to cool slightly; drain and cool the carrots. Add to the tuna fish, season with salt and freshly ground black pepper, and blend in the mayonnaise. Spoon half the mixture into a serving dish, put the halved eggs on top, and then the remaining tuna and rice mixture. Top with peanuts and parsley. Cover and chill until needed.

Beef and Spaghetti Winter Warmer *(serves 6)*

1 onion, finely chopped	Squeeze of lemon juice
1 clove garlic, crushed	1 green pepper, seeded and
2 tablespoons cooking oil	chopped
1 lb (450 g) minced beef	1 carrot, peeled and grated
6 rashers lean bacon, derinded	4 oz (125 g) garlic sausage,
and chopped	skinned and chopped
1 x 14 oz (400 g) can tomatoes,	Salt and freshly ground black
roughly chopped	pepper
1 pt (500 ml) beef stock	Paprika
2 tablespoons tomato purée	1 x 15 oz (425 g) can spaghetti in
2 teaspoons sugar	tomato sauce

Fry the chopped onion and crushed garlic gently in a large, heavy saucepan with the oil until soft and transparent. Add the mince and bacon and cook until lightly browned. Add the canned tomatoes, stock, tomato purée, sugar and lemon juice; bring to the boil and simmer for 10 minutes.

Toss in the green pepper, carrot and garlic sausage, and season to taste with salt, pepper and as much paprika as you think the family can bear. Simmer for a further 15–20 minutes. Then add the canned spaghetti and stir well. Pour into a wide-mouthed flask and serve as a complete main course with fresh crusty bread or with baked potatoes.

Savoury Loaf in Bacon *(serves 6)*

1 lb (450 g) raw, best quality	1 tablespoon parsley, chopped
minced beef	1 tablespoon tomato chutney
4 oz (125 g) sausage meat	or ketchup
4 oz (125 g) fresh white	Salt and freshly ground black
breadcrumbs	pepper
1 onion, finely chopped	2 eggs
1 teaspoon Worcestershire sauce	6 rashers streaky bacon

Place all the ingredients, except the eggs and bacon, in a large mixing bowl and mix thoroughly. Beat the eggs and stir them in also.

Remove the rind from the bacon rashers and stretch them with the back of a knife. Use the bacon to line a greased 2 lb (900 g) loaf tin. Press the meat mixture into the tin and cook in a moderate oven (375°F, 190°C; Gas Mark 5) for 1 hour.

When cooked, remove from the oven and leave to cool in the tin. Turn out when cold, cut in slices and wrap in foil.

Gammon Cooked in Cider *(serves up to 10)*

3 lb (1.4 kg) gammon	Bouquet garni
1¾ pints (1 l) cider	2 tablespoons brown sugar
Cloves	

Soak the gammon for at least 4 hours if smoked, 2 if unsmoked. If you dislike salt, soak overnight.

Place the gammon in a saucepan just big enough to hold it. Add the cider to cover, 6 whole cloves and the bouquet garni. Bring to the boil, then cover and simmer for about 1¼ hours, turning the meat occasionally in the apple stock. When cooked, remove from the pan and strip off the skin, leaving just a thin layer of fat. Place joint in a roasting tin with the largest expanse of fat uppermost. Score in a diamond pattern, coat with the brown sugar and decorate with cloves.

Bake in a hot oven (425°F, 220°C; Gas Mark 7) for 15-20 minutes, until the skin is crisp and brown. Allow to cool. If you do not intend carving at the picnic site, slice now, before wrapping in foil.

Cheese, Ham and Mushroom Flan *(serves 4–6)*

6 oz (175 g) plain flour	2 oz (50 g) onion, peeled and
Pinch of salt	chopped
Pinch of mustard powder	4 oz (125 g) ham, diced
1½ oz (40 g) margarine	2 oz (50 g) mushrooms, finely
1½ oz (40 g) lard	chopped
Cold water	3 oz (75 g) Cheddar cheese,
Beaten egg to glaze	grated
	2 eggs
For the filling:	2 tablespoons single cream
½ oz (15 g) butter	Pinch of nutmeg

To make the pastry, sift the flour, salt and mustard powder. Blend in the margarine and lard until the mixture resembles fine breadcrumbs. Add a teaspoon of cold water to the beaten egg and use some of this mixture to bind the pastry. Roll out thinly and line an 8 in (20 cm) flan case. Prick the base with a fork, place on a baking sheet and brush sides with remaining egg and water mixture. Bake 'blind' in a hot oven (400°F, 200°C; Gas Mark 6) for 15 minutes, uncovering the pastry for the last 5 minutes.

To make the filling, fry the onion gently in the butter to soften; add diced ham and chopped mushrooms and cook for a few minutes more. Leave to cool. Spoon the ham, onion and mushroom mixture into the base of the flan case. Cover with grated cheese. Beat eggs and cream together with the pinch of nutmeg, and pour into the flan case. Bake in a moderately hot oven (375°F, 190°C; Gas Mark 5) for about 35–40 minutes until set. Allow to cool and cover with clingfilm or foil.

Crispy Chicken with Oriental Sauce *(serves 4)*

3 oz (75 g) butter or margarine
6 oz (175 g) fresh white
  breadcrumbs
Finely grated rind of 1 orange
4 chicken portions, skinned
Salt and pepper
1 egg, beaten

For Oriental Sauce:
1 medium onion, chopped
1 tablespoon cooking oil

8 oz (225 g) can of apricot halves
Juice of 1 orange
2 teaspoons Worcestershire
  sauce
2 tablespoons white wine vinegar
1 tablespoon Demerara sugar
Salt and white pepper
1 teaspoon arrowroot
2 tablespoons water
Watercress sprigs to garnish

Melt the butter slowly in a large saucepan or mixing bowl; mix in the breadcrumbs and grated orange rind. Dry the chicken thoroughly with kitchen paper, season with salt and pepper, and dip into the beaten egg. Toss the chicken pieces in the breadcrumb mix and make sure they are well covered. Place on a baking sheet and cook in a moderate oven (375°F, 190°C; Gas Mark 5) for 1 1/4 hours.

To make the sauce, cook the onion gently in the oil until soft and transparent. Chop the apricot halves and add to the onion along with their juice and that of the orange, the Worcestershire sauce, vinegar, sugar and seasoning. Bring to the boil and simmer gently for about 5 minutes. Blend arrowroot and water, add to the pan and cook, stirring, until thickened and smooth. Allow chicken and sauce to cool. Serve separately with potato crisps, green salad and a rice salad.

Double Bubbles *(serves 4)*

8 cottage-loaf shaped rolls (or
  similar)
Butter for spreading
2 eggs, scrambled
2 rashers bacon, derinded, fried
  crisp and chopped

4 spring onions
4 oz (125 g) liver pâté
1/2 small lettuce
4 tomatoes, sliced
8 stuffed olives, sliced
Fresh parsley, chopped

17

Cut 2 pockets, one above the other, in each roll. Spread plenty of butter on all the cut surfaces.

Mix together the scrambled eggs and crisp bacon, and spread in the top pockets of four of the rolls. Slice the spring onions, mix with the liver paté, and spread in the top pockets of the other four.

Cut the lettuce leaves into strips, combine with the sliced tomatoes and olives and sprinkle with chopped parsley. Stuff the bottom pockets of the rolls with this salad mixture.

Wrap in foil and chill briefly before departure. These rolls must be prepared on the day of the picnic.

Barbecue Brainwaves
Instead of plain burgers in a sesame seed bap, try slotting homemade hamburgers into pitta bread with a dressed salad of shredded lettuce, tomato strips, grated onion, diced cucumber and Feta cheese. Try Mexican burgers with refried beans and Taco sauce inside pitta; or cheesy-onion burgers, with chopped spring onions, mushrooms, bacon and sour cream, topped with a melting slice of Swiss cheese.

As a change from the inevitable garlic bread, try sprinkling dried thyme onto well-buttered French bread and wrapping it in foil.

Delicious though the taste of charcoal cooking is, it needs good marinades and sauces to bring it to life and add variety. Here are some ideas, plus a couple of desserts.

Chicken and Courgettes with Lime and Ginger
Take chicken breasts, skin and bone them and cut into chunks. Marinate in the juice of 3 or 4 limes blended with 1 level teaspoon of ground ginger. Thread on a skewer with sliced courgettes, mushrooms and green pepper. Place on an oiled grill.

Florida Chicken
Marinate chicken pieces in ¼ pt (150 ml) dry white wine, 1 tablespoon soy sauce, 1 clove of garlic, crushed, and the juice of 1 orange and 1 grapefruit. Brush the chicken with melted butter before cooking and accompany with grilled orange, tomato and grapefruit.

Mock Tandoori
Soak pieces of chicken or lamb in ½ pt (250 ml) natural yoghurt, juice of a lemon and 2 teaspoons turmeric for 48 hours. Cook with plenty of fat bacon and serve with a salad of chopped onion, tomato and cucumber flavoured with mint sauce and chilli powder.

Shashlik of Salmon
Soak chunks of raw, skinned salmon in the juice of two lemons, salt

and freshly ground black pepper. Dip the drained fish first in flour, then beaten egg, then in breadcrumbs. Thread on a skewer alternately with sliced mushrooms and segments of lemon.

Fish Parcel
Marinate a whole fish, such as sea bass, bream or salmon trout in ½ pt (250 ml) dry white wine, juice of 2 lemons, chopped onion, parsley and fennel. Wrap fish and marinade in double-strength foil and leave for a few hours in the refrigerator. Open the parcel before placing on the barbecue.

Sweet and Sour Apricot Ribs
Simmer pork spare ribs until just tender in the comfort of your own kitchen. Then marinate in a sauce of 4 oz (125 g) puréed apricots, 2 tablespoons apricot brandy, 3 fl oz (75 ml) white wine vinegar, 2 tablespoons soy sauce, 4 oz (125 g) brown sugar, 1 crushed clove garlic and ½ teaspoon ground ginger. Drain well, cook over hot coals and baste during the cooking.

Steak and Stilton
Marinate thick steaks in oil and vinegar, salt and freshly ground black pepper. Drain, cut almost in half and insert a slice of Stilton cheese. Before cooking, brush with melted parsley butter.

Sausages in Sage and Honey
Marinate 1 lb (450 g) good pork sausages in 4 tablespoons thin honey, grated onion, juice of 1 orange, and 1 teaspoon powdered sage. Serve with sharp mustard.

Lemon-herbed Vegetable Kebab
Soak chunks of tomato, mushroom, courgette, green pepper and pineapple in a dressing made from the juice of 2 lemons, 1 tablespoon caster sugar, pinch of salt, 1 bay leaf, chopped parsley and tarragon. Thread on a skewer and cook, basting occasionally with butter.

Spicy Tomato Barbecue Sauce
Blend together in a saucepan ¼ pt (150 ml) bottled tomato sauce, 2 tablespoons vinegar, 1 tablespoon Worcestershire sauce, 1 tablespoon grated onion, 2 tablespoons cooking oil, 1 oz (25 g) butter, 1 teaspoon sugar, 1 teaspoon salt, ½ teaspoon garlic powder, 1 teaspoon paprika, ½ teaspoon mixed spice and ½ teaspoon dry mustard. Bring the mixture to the boil and simmer over a low heat for about 10 minutes.

Rum and Raisin Apples

Remove core and cut skin around the centre of each cooking apple. Fill the centre with a mixture of 2 oz (50 g) raisins, 4 tablespoons rum and 4 oz (125 g) soft brown sugar. Top with a generous knob of butter, and barbecue, wrapped in foil.

Brandied Bananas

Lay bananas on a sheet of foil, and spoon over 2 tablespoons of brandy, 4 tablespoons soft brown sugar and ½ teaspoon cinnamon. Dot with butter and enclose completely in foil.

Potato and Watercress Salad *(serves 4)*

1 lb (450 g) new potatoes	*For the dressing:*
2 tablespoons spring onions, chopped	3 tablespoons oil
	2 tablespoons mayonnaise
Bunch of watercress	2 teaspoons wine vinegar
	Salt and freshly ground black pepper

Scrub the potatoes and cook them in their skins until just tender. Drain and slice into a bowl whilst still hot. Sprinkle the chopped spring onions on top. Strip the leaves from the watercress and chop finely, add to the potato and onion.

Make up the dressing in a screw-top jar and pour over the salad while it is warm. Stir to coat thoroughly and leave to cool. To transport, spoon salad into a rigid plastic container and keep cool.

Bramble Crunch *(serves 4–6)*

1 lb (450 g) blackberries	8 oz (225 g) digestive biscuits
1 tablespoon water	4 oz (125 g) Demerara sugar
Caster sugar	¼ pt (150 ml) whipped cream

Cook the blackberries with the water until soft, and sweeten to taste with caster sugar. Crush the digestive biscuits with a rolling pin and mix with the Demerara sugar. Place alternate layers of biscuit and blackberries into individual serving dishes or yoghurt pots. Top with whipped cream, cover with clingfilm and serve chilled.

Peach and Mincemeat Pie *(serves 4–6)*

8 oz (225 g) plain flour	1 tablespoon lemon juice
¼ teaspoon salt	4–5 fresh peaches
2 oz (50 g) lard	3 level tablespoons mincemeat
4 oz (125 g) butter	Beaten egg to glaze
1 oz (25 g) caster sugar	Caster sugar for sprinkling
1 egg yolk, beaten	

Sieve the flour and salt together. Rub in first the lard, then the butter until the mixture resembles breadcrumbs. Toss in the sugar and mix thoroughly. Beat the egg and a dessertspoon of lemon juice together. Add to the pastry mix and blend to a smooth dough. Knead briefly, cover and leave to rest in the refrigerator for about ½ hour.

Meanwhile, skin and stone the peaches and slice into segments. Place in a bowl, along with the mincemeat and remaining lemon juice.

Roll out the pastry and line a 9 in (23 cm) pie plate. Fill with peaches and mincemeat and cover with remaining pastry, making sure that you seal the edges carefully by brushing first with water. Cut a hole in the top and brush with beaten egg. Bake in a moderate oven (375°F, 190°C; Gas Mark 5) for 40 minutes.

Allow to cool; sprinkle the top of the pie with caster sugar and encase in foil. Serve either cold or warmed on the barbecue.

Fruit and Nut Gingerbread

4 oz (125 g) butter or margarine	1 teaspoon mixed spice
6 oz (175 g) black treacle	1 tablespoon ground ginger
2 oz (50 g) golden syrup	2 oz (50 g) caster sugar
¼ pt (150 ml) milk	2 oz (50 g) sultanas
2 eggs, beaten	1 oz (25 g) walnuts or almonds,
8 oz (225 g) plain flour	chopped
1 teaspoon bicarbonate of soda	

Put the butter, treacle and golden syrup into a large saucepan and mix together over a low heat. Add the milk, mix thoroughly, and allow to cool. Blend eggs into the syrup mixture.

Sift together the flour, bicarbonate of soda, mixed spice and ground ginger in a large mixing bowl. Add the sugar and mix thoroughly. Make a well in the centre of the dry mixture and pour in the syrup. Gradually draw in flour around the well and blend to form a smooth batter. Stir in the sultanas and nuts and turn into a greased and lined 7 in (18 cm) square cake tin. Bake on the middle shelf of a slow oven (300°F, 150°C; Gas Mark 2) for 1¼ hours. Cool in the tin for 5–10 minutes before turning out. Wrap in foil when completely cold.

Orange Cut and Come Again Cake

8 oz (225 g) self-raising flour	2 oz (50 g) chopped nuts
1 level teaspoon baking powder	Finely grated rind of 2 oranges
Pinch of salt	*For Orange Butter filling:*
½ teaspoon mixed spice	2 oz (50 g) soft butter
8 oz (225 g) curd cheese	8 oz (225 g) icing sugar, sieved
6 oz (175 g) soft brown sugar	Juice of 1 orange
3 eggs	

Sieve the flour, baking powder, salt and mixed spice together. In a separate bowl, beat the curd cheese and sugar together. Beat in the eggs one at a time. Stir in the chopped nuts, the orange rind, and fold in the dry ingredients.

Line a 2 lb (900 g) loaf tin with greaseproof paper, pile in the mixture, and bake in the top half of a moderate oven (350°F, 180°C; Gas Mark 4) for about 50 minutes until risen and lightly brown. Leave to cool in the tin for 10 minutes, then remove and peel off the greaseproof paper. Cool on a wire rack.

To make the orange butter, cream the butter lightly, beating in the icing sugar a little at a time and adding the orange juice to give a smooth icing that is easy to spread.

Slice the cake lengthwise and sandwich the two halves together with the orange butter. Wrap in foil until required.

Lemon Barley Water *(serves 4–6)*

3 lemons	2 pt (1.25 l) water
4 oz (125 g) caster sugar	3 tablespoons pearl barley

Wash the lemons, dry them and pare the rind finely. Squeeze the lemon juice and strain it into a large jug. Place the rind in a large mixing bowl with the sugar.

Bring the water to boil with the pearl barley in a large saucepan. Cover and simmer slowly for 10 minutes, then pour into the mixing bowl containing rind and sugar. Allow to cool before straining into the jug and mixing with the lemon juice.

Chill for a few hours, then pour into a large vacuum flask containing a few ice cubes.

Iced Coffee with a Kick *(serves 4)*

1 pt (500 ml) strong black coffee	¼ pt (150 ml) whipped cream or
Sugar to taste	ice cream
Ice cubes	Rum, whisky or brandy to taste

Make the coffee in your usual way, remembering to make it extra strong. While still hot, stir in the amount of sugar the family will agree on (a couple of tablespoons is usually enough—it can be added later to the cup, but will not dissolve very well in the cold liquid). Allow to cool before pouring into a thermos flask with a handful of ice cubes.

If using ice cream you will have to carry it to the picnic site in a wide-mouthed vacuum flask; if using whipped cream it should survive if kept in a rigid plastic container in a cooled ice box.

To serve, pour black coffee and ice into each cup; add spirits according to taste, for those who are allowed them, and top with a dollop of whipped cream or ice cream.

CHILDREN'S PICNICS

For the most part, children's preferences in food are simple, popularly conventional and utterly lacking in what adults might call 'taste'. Ask anyone who has spent long hours preparing a homemade soup or chutney, only to be told by an infant that the mass-produced, psychedelic-coloured variety is infinitely preferable.

As far as picnics go, children, given the choice, will plump for the foods and drinks they know best. Crisps, chocolate, apples, yoghurts and, for some reason, pork pies rank as children's favourites. One or two of the more adventurous—or dissatisfied, depending on which way you look at it—may opt for the unusual. Cold fish fingers are not everyone's idea of a picnic delicacy but they do, believe it or not, find favour in some quarters. So does garlic sausage eaten on its own in great hunks, and cold rice pudding spooned straight from the tin.

Children in Victorian times had none of the instant food that we have today, and yet a list of their provisions for a picnic tea makes mouth-watering reading. From Stella Austin's *Stumps* there is apple tart, mulberry tart, plum cake, sponge cake, biscuits, shortbread, macaroons, quantities of bread and butter, hard-boiled eggs, plums, pears and greengages.

Even picnics described in children's books written this century, but before the advent of the hamburger and hot dog, have a dated air about them: Frances Hodgson Burnett's *The Secret Garden*, published in 1911, describes all manner of picnics for the two outcasts, Mary and Colin. They dip into pails of rich, new milk, eat hot cottage-made currant buns from blue and white napkins, and roast eggs and potatoes in a home-built oven. Not a crisp or a bottle of pop in sight!

Mole and Ratty's picnic in *The Wind in the Willows* dates from much the same time:

'What's inside it?' asked the Mole, wriggling with curiosity.

'There's cold chicken inside it' replied the Rat briefly; 'cold tongue-coldhamcoldbeefpickledgherkinssaladfrenchrollscresssandwiches-pottedmeatgingerbeerlemonadesodawater–'

'O stop, stop,' cried the Mole in ecstasies: 'This is too much!'

How many children today would enjoy all those cold meats, be impressed by cress sandwiches or even know what homemade ginger beer tasted like?

Perhaps saddest of all, and worth remembering in these days of

23

plenty, is Maud Pember Reeves' account of working-class poverty in Lambeth during the Twenties. In her book *Round About A Pound A Week* she records:

> In holiday-time elder brothers and sisters sometimes organise a party to Kennington Park or one of the open spaces nearby, and the grass becomes a shrieking mass of children, from twelve or thirteen years of age downwards. The weary mother gives them bread and margarine in a piece of newspaper, and there is always a fountain from which they can drink.

If escapism is the spark behind adult picnics, for children it is the guiding star. In Arthur Ransome's famous *Swallows and Amazons* series, adventures and picnics spill from every page. One minute it is a native-style birthday party with a pink and white iced cake and a bunch of bananas tied to a tree (as if it was growing there); the next, an igloo feast or a tin of pemmican, or cook's rations consisting of ginger biscuits, apple pie, toffee fudge and black sticky cake. The fact that these books were written in the Twenties and Thirties matters not a bit for they manage to convey the excitement and magnetic appeal of outdoor living in a way that few books do, or try to do, these days. Just one picnic from *Swallowdale* serves as an example:

> Cook had given them a fat beef roll, like a bigger and better kind of sausage. There were enough apple dumplings to go round. There were lettuces and radishes and salt in a little tin box. There was a lot of cut brown bread and butter. There was a hunk, the sort of hunk that really is a hunk, a hunk big enough for twelve indoor people and just right for six sailors, of the blackest and juiciest and stickiest fruit cake. And then to wash these good things down, there was the bedroom jug full of pirate grog, which some people might have thought was lemonade. Lemonade or grog, whatever it was, it suited thirsty throats.

Just how you inject a little magic into your child's picnic depends to a certain extent on the time at your disposal. Undoubtedly it is worth spending hours decorating cakes with funny faces or boats or whatever, but if time is short the judicious use of a few Smarties or chocolate curls can do just as well. The point being that some decoration is better than none at all.

The excitement conveyed by a Ransome picnic owes as much to the choice of location or timing as it does to the actual food. If cherished picnic spots are crowded at lunchtime, why not make it a picnic tea, or even better, a picnic breakfast, as in Dorothy Edwards' tale of *My Naughty Little Sister and the Chimney Sweep*. Exercise the full stretch of your imagination in the packing of the picnic—to avoid squabbles individual boxes are best, but each one could be wrapped in bright colours and named, or shrouded in mysterious brown paper with a secret message to find. As well as food, include little treats such as a name badge, a colouring book and pencils, a simple puzzle or a small toy.

24

Give your party a theme if it is a special occasion. It could be a Mad Hatter's Tea Party or a Mr Men picnic. Remember the success of the greatest picnicker of all time, the Teddy Bear. Since the song 'The Teddy Bears' Picnic' first appeared in 1930, the sum total of its many versions is said to be in excess of 20 million copies. More recently Yogi (famed for his devotion to honey and pies in Yellowstone Park) and Paddington (marmalade sandwiches) have kept the theme alive. Now an annual gathering of Teddy Bear lovers (or arctophiles as they call themselves) takes place every year at Longleat in Wiltshire. A high point of the event is a regular Teddy Bears' Picnic with marmalade sandwiches and honey cakes.

However, children, unlike bears, do not always appreciate a picnic packed full of tooth-rotting, sweet things. Many, even the tiny ones, actually prefer savouries, with cheese in any shape or form coming well up the list. The accent should be on variety, on plenty of colour to catch the eye, and on portions small enough to leave room for many more besides. Of course it is a meal and as such should in some way be nourishing; but if this can be done without the appearance of 'good, solid food', then so much the better.

Cheddar Gorge *(serves 6–8)*

4 oz (125 g) good quality butter
2 oz (50 g) cottage cheese, sieved
½ teaspoon white wine vinegar
8 oz (225 g) Cheddar cheese, grated

Salt and freshly ground black pepper
1 tablespoon chopped chives (optional)

Cream the butter, add the sieved cottage cheese and mix well. Add the vinegar and mix again thoroughly. Gradually add the grated Cheddar cheese.

Season to taste with salt and pepper and fold in the chopped chives. Spoon the pâté mixture into a pretty dish, cover with greaseproof paper and chill. Serve with salty crackers or small digestive biscuits.

Fisherman's Fancies *(makes 6–8)*

4 eggs
1 tablespoon arrowroot
4 fl oz (100 ml) top of the milk
1 x 10 oz (300 g) can condensed mushroom soup

2 tablespoons lemon juice
7 oz (200 g) tinned tuna or sardines, drained, skinned, boned and flaked
1 large packet of crisps, crushed

Hard boil the eggs and chop them roughly. Dissolve the arrowroot in the milk, stir into the soup along with the lemon juice, and heat, mixing thoroughly.

Add the eggs and the flaked fish to the soup mixture; stir, then add half the crushed crisps. Divide the mixture between 6–8 ramekin dishes. Allow to cool, chill in the refrigerator, then sprinkle the remaining crushed crisps on top.

Serve cold or reheated, together with Marmite Twists—strips of cheese pastry that are twisted, baked and sandwiched together with marmite.

Beefies in Pitta *(serves 4–6)*

8 oz (225 g) good-quality minced beef	½ teaspoon salt
	Freshly ground black pepper
1 small onion, chopped	Pinch of marjoram
2 tablespoons fresh parsley, chopped	1 teaspoon chopped mint
	Pitta bread
2 tablespoons tomato ketchup	

Mix the beef, onion, parsley, ketchup, salt, pepper, marjoram and mint together in a bowl. Leave to rest in the refrigerator for about ½ hour so that the flavours can mingle.

Make into flat cakes, dust with flour and fry well on either side. Serve hot, if possible, inside buttered pitta bread. However, these beef cakes taste just as good when cold.

Spag and Porky Pies *(makes about 16 pies)*

8 oz (225 g) plain flour	1 egg yolk
Large pinch of salt	2 teaspoons cold water
Cayenne pepper	Small can spaghetti hoops
4 oz (125 g) butter or margarine	2 frankfurter sausages, chopped
3 oz (75 g) Cheddar cheese, finely grated	Salt and pepper
	Beaten egg to glaze

To make the cheese pastry, sift together the flour, salt and a dash of cayenne pepper. Rub in the fat until the mixture resembles fine breadcrumbs. Add 2 oz (50 g) of the grated cheese and mix thoroughly. Blend the egg yolk and water in a cup; add to the mixture and mix to a firm dough.

Roll out the pastry thinly and line some individual patty tins (mince-pie size). Mix the spaghetti with the chopped frankfurters and remaining grated cheese, and season to taste. Spoon into the pastry cases, and cover with pastry lids, remembering to damp and seal the edges. Brush with beaten egg and bake in a hot oven (400°F, 200°C; Gas Mark 6) for about 15–20 minutes.

These pies are really tasty and can be served either hot or cold. Wrap them in foil to protect the pastry crust.

Pemmican Roll *(serves 4–6)*

1 oz (25 g) butter or margarine
1 medium onion, chopped
4 tomatoes, skinned, seeded and
  chopped
1 x 12 oz (350 g) can corned beef,
  diced

Large pinch of mixed herbs
1 teaspoon Worcestershire sauce
Salt and freshly ground black
  pepper
8 oz (225 g) puff pastry
Beaten egg to glaze

Heat the butter in a saucepan and gently fry the onion until soft. Add
the tomatoes and fry for a few minutes more. Stir in the corned beef,
herbs and sauce. Cook gently for 5 minutes and season to taste. Allow
to cool.

Roll out the pastry to an oblong shape, approximately 12 x 8 in (30
x 20 cm). Spoon the corned beef mixture down the centre of the
pastry. Moisten the pastry edges and fold the longest edges into the
middle. Seal the ends in parcel fashion.

Place roll on a baking sheet with the join underneath. Brush the top
with beaten egg and make a few slits along the top. Bake in a moderately hot oven (400°F, 200°C; Gas Mark 6) for 20 minutes or until the
pastry is cooked and golden brown.

Allow to cool, cut into slices and wrap in foil.

Crunchy Coleslaw and Frankfurters *(serves 6–8)*

1 x 15 oz (425 g) can frankfurters
1 red-skinned eating apple
1 tablespoon lemon juice
1 oz (25 g) Cheddar cheese, cubed
1 oz (25 g) raisins
1 oz (25 g) walnuts, roughly
  chopped

2 sticks celery, chopped
8 oz (225 g) white cabbage, finely
  shredded
2 tablespoons mayonnaise
1 tablespoon single cream or
  top of the milk
Salt and pepper

Slice the frankfurters into bite-sized pieces. Core and chop the apple
and dip in lemon juice. Add apple and sliced sausage to the cheese,
raisins, walnuts, celery and cabbage and mix well.

Combine the mayonnaise and the cream, add the salt and pepper
and pour over the salad. Pile into individual plastic dishes with lids
(yoghurt or cottage-cheese pots are ideal) and keep cool until required. With marmite sandwiches or buttered crispbread, this is a
meal in itself.

Cheesy Sausages *(serves 6)*

6 large pork sausages
6 slices Leicester cheese, halved
  lengthwise

6 rashers streaky bacon

Slit the sausages lengthwise and put 2 half slices of cheese in each. Snip the rind from the bacon and stretch each rasher with a knife. Wrap round the sausage and cheese and secure with a cocktail stick.

Lay the rolls out on a baking sheet or roasting tin and bake in a moderately hot oven (400°F, 200°C; Gas Mark 6) for about 40 minutes. Drain on kitchen paper, then wrap in foil. Keep warm in a biscuit tin lined with rolled-up newspaper or pop the cooled sausages in the refrigerator and serve chilled.

Castaway Salad *(serves 6–8)*

12 oz (350 g) cooked, cold meat (chicken, ham, garlic sausage or corned beef)	1 level tablespoon desiccated coconut
12 oz (350 g) pineapple chunks, drained	4 tablespoons mayonnaise
1 level tablespoon raisins	Large leaves of cos lettuce
1 level teaspoon curry powder	1 tablespoon chopped chives
	Sliced tomatoes to garnish

Dice the cooked meat and put into a basin with the pineapple chunks, raisins, curry powder, coconut and mayonnaise. Toss together until all the ingredients are well coated with mayonnaise.

Trim the cos leaves (1 for each picnicker) and lay them lengthwise in 2 plastic ice-cream containers. Spoon the salad mixture into each lettuce 'boat' and sprinkle with chopped chives. Accompany with sliced tomatoes and keep chilled until required.

Sandwich Kebabs *(serves 4–6)*

4 thin slices white bread, buttered	12 maraschino cherries, halved
4 thin slices brown bread, buttered	3 gherkins, quartered
4 different but compatible sandwich fillings (eg ham and cheese slices; chicken and shrimp paste)	12 small cubes of cheese
	12 cocktail sticks

Make four sandwiches, each with a thin slice of brown and white bread and one of the four fillings. Remove the crusts and cut each sandwich into three equal lengths, then each length into three again to make 9 squares of about 1 in (2.5 cm).

Thread half a cherry on one end of the stick, then a sandwich cube, then a piece of gherkin, then another sandwich of a different flavour, then a cube of cheese, then a further, different flavoured, sandwich cube, and finally the other half of cherry. Repeat this procedure with the remaining cocktail sticks.

Lay the kebabs in a greaseproof-lined sandwich box and serve chilled if possible.

Cornflake and Honey Cakes *(makes 18–20)*

2 oz (50 g) butter or margarine
2 oz (50 g) sugar
1 tablespoon orange juice
Finely grated rind of ½ small
   orange

1 tablespoon honey
4 oz (125 g) cornflakes
Chocolate vermicelli to decorate

Put the buter, sugar, orange juice, rind and honey into a saucepan and bring to the boil gently. Simmer for about 2 minutes.

Remove from the heat and stir in the cornflakes. Spoon into small paper cases and bake in a moderate oven (350°F, 180°C; Gas Mark 4) for 5 minutes. Allow to cool partially before decorating with chocolate vermicelli. Pack into a rigid container.

Scandinavian Rings *(makes about 10–12 rings)*

6 oz (175 g) puff pastry
1 egg, beaten
2 oz (50 g) granulated sugar
2 oz (50 g) butter or margarine

3 oz (75 g) icing sugar
1 egg yolk
½ teaspoon vanilla essence

Roll out the pastry to about ⅛ in (3 mm) thick and, using 2 sizes of pastry cutter, stamp out rings of the dough about 2½ in (6.5 cm) in diameter. Lay the rings on a baking sheet, brush with beaten egg and sprinkle granulated sugar on top. Bake in a hot oven (425°F, 220°C; Gas Mark 7) for 8–10 minutes.

Allow to cool on a wire rack while you prepare the butter icing. Cream the butter and add the icing sugar gradually. Beat until the filling is smooth and creamy. Beat in the egg yolk and the vanilla essence.

Sandwich the cooled rings together, spreading butter icing on the non-glazed side of each ring. Pack into a rigid container.

Hedgehogs *(makes 16–18)*

6 oz (175 g) butter or margarine
4 oz (125 g) caster sugar
3 eggs
4 oz (125 g) self-raising flour

1 teaspoon baking powder
4 oz (125 g) plain chocolate
6 oz (175 g) icing sugar, sifted
A few currants

Put 4 oz (125 g) butter, the caster sugar, 2 eggs, sifted flour and baking powder into a mixing bowl. Beat together until the mixture is smooth and glossy.

Thoroughly grease some round-bottomed mince-pie tins. Spoon the mixture into the tins, levelling the top with the back of a spoon. Bake in a very moderate oven (325°F, 160°C; Gas Mark 3) for about 20 minutes. Loosen the cakes with a palette knife and gently prise them out to cool on a wire rack. When cool, trim one side of each cake to form a pointed 'snout'.

To make the icing, break up the chocolate and melt it in a bowl over water. Cream the remaining 2 oz (50 g) butter with the remaining egg. Sift in the icing sugar gradually, then beat in the chocolate.

Spread this over the upside-down cakes, leaving a thick 'roughcast' effect and pulling the icing with the back of a spoon to form peaks, resembling the hedgehog's spikes. Stick currants in place to look like eyes and noses.

Leave the hedgehogs to harden in the refrigerator for at least a couple of hours. Pack them carefully into rigid plastic containers and avoid long bumpy journeys.

Ginger Beer

1 lemon
1 oz (25 g) root ginger, bruised
1 lb (450 g) sugar
1 oz (25 g) cream of tartar

8 pt (4.5 l) water
1 oz (25 g) fresh yeast (or 4
  teaspoons dried yeast)

Peel the lemon and squeeze its juice. Strain the juice and put it into a large bowl or clean plastic bucket along with the rind, ginger, sugar and cream of tartar. Boil the water and pour over the sugar and ginger. Stir well and leave until tepid before adding the yeast.

Leave the mixture overnight to ferment. Then skim off the yeast and pour the ginger beer into screw-topped bottles. Leave for 2–3 days before drinking.

Strawberry Milk Shake *(serves 4–6)*

1 pt (500 ml) milk
½ family-size block strawberry
  ice cream

8 oz (225 g) fresh strawberries,
  crushed

Put half the milk and half the ice cream in the blender and liquidise thoroughly. Repeat with the remaining milk and ice cream.

Pour the mixture into a 2 pt (1.25 l) jug and add the crushed strawberries. Mix well and pour into a pre-chilled vacuum jug. Fill to the brim with extra milk or a few ice cubes.

SPORTING PICNICS

There is nothing so democratic as a sporting picnic. It matters not whether you are a lord or a labourer, a countess or a charlady, you can still enjoy your portable provisions and your favourite pastime in the way that nature intended. Of course the style and location of your picnic will vary in accordance with your pocket and inclination. But the inestimable rewards are there just the same, be it a sumptuous banquet in a shady meadow or a simple 'thumber' (a racegoer's description for a thumbpiece of meat with bread) on a windswept heath.

In England it is the time of the year which dictates what provisions you take on your sporting picnic. We have two seasons, climatically speaking, winter and summer, and even then the latter has been known to bear a marked resemblance to the former. All this would account for the paramount need to take victuals of a warming nature—not hot, necessarily, just warming—and this possibly explains why the presence of alcohol is so important.

In years gone by, when winters were colder and summers hotter (so we are told) it was undoubtedly the booze that kept picnickers going. What else could explain the enormous quantity of drink—36 quart bottles of ale, sherry, claret and soft drinks, plus an unspecified quantity of champagne and light wine—suggested for Mrs Beeton's picnic of 40 people? Had they had thermos flasks and hot soup perhaps the whole affair would have been as abstemious as a Sunday-school outing.

By far the best-known sporting picnics are those that accompany the shooting party. Originally, when shooting was a sport for farmers and yeomen, these were modest meals—a crust of bread with cheese, a few biscuits and a flask of ale, perhaps. Then, in the mid-nineteenth century, the gentlemen took over the sport and suddenly the performance of lunch became a much grander affair. In *The Big Shots*, Jonathan Garnier Ruffer describes how inestimable care went into the preparation of the Edwardian shooting lunch, particularly if King Edward VII, or 'The Presence' as he was known, happened to be there. On many occasions a special marquee would be erected, or an elegant table laid out with the table linen, silver and china from the main house. Extra guests might be invited, and a meal of five courses, lasting an hour and a half, would be served.

And the food! Oysters, lobsters, foie gras, plovers' eggs and devilled

BILL OF FARE FOR A PICNIC FOR 40 PERSONS.

2149. A joint of cold roast beef, a joint of cold boiled beef, 2 ribs of lamb, 2 shoulders of lamb, 4 roast fowls, 2 roast ducks, 1 ham, 1 tongue, 2 veal-and-ham pies, 2 pigeon pies, 6 medium-sized lobsters, 1 piece of collared calf's head, 18 lettuces, 6 baskets of salad, 6 cucumbers.

2150. Stewed fruit well sweetened, and put into glass bottles well corked ; 3 or 4 dozen plain pastry biscuits to eat with the stewed fruit, 2 dozen fruit turnovers, 4 dozen cheesecakes, 2 cold cabinet puddings in moulds, 2 blanc-manges in moulds, a few jam puffs, 1 large cold plum-pudding (this must be good), a few baskets of fresh fruit, 3 dozen plain biscuits, a piece of cheese, 6 lbs. of butter (this, of course, includes the butter for tea), 4 quartern loaves of household bread, 3 dozen rolls, 6 loaves of tin bread (for tea), 2 plain plum cakes, 2 pound cakes, 2 sponge cakes, a tin of mixed biscuits, $\frac{1}{2}$ lb. of tea. Coffee is not suitable for a picnic, being difficult to make.

Things not to be forgotten at a Picnic.

2151. A stick of horseradish, a bottle of mint-sauce well corked, a bottle of salad dressing, a bottle of vinegar, made mustard, pepper, salt, good oil, and pounded sugar. If it can be managed, take a little ice. It is scarcely necessary to say that plates, tumblers, wine-glasses, knives, forks, and spoons, must not be forgotten ; as also teacups and saucers, 3 or 4 teapots, some lump sugar, and milk, if this last-named article cannot be obtained in the neighbourhood. Take 3 corkscrews.

2152. *Beverages.*—3 dozen quart bottles of ale, packed in hampers; ginger-beer, soda-water, and lemonade, of each 2 dozen bottles ; 6 bottles of sherry, 6 bottles of claret, champagne à discrétion, and any other light wine that may be preferred, and 2 bottles of brandy. Water can usually be obtained ∙ so it is useless to take it.

An extract from an early edition of Mrs Beeton's *Book of Household Management*

larks might precede a whole roast loin of pork or a dish of jugged wild duck, kept hot in silver dishes with spirit lamps beneath. Exquisite champagnes would chase the food down, with trifles, jellies and exotic hot-house fruits to follow. Finally, liqueurs—usually port, brandy or madeira—would follow the cheese. No wonder Albert, the Prince Consort, ordained that there should be no shooting in the afternoon (a practice not followed by Edward VII who continued to blast away until dusk).

Today shooting-party picnics are of a more practical nature. Now that the guns can be ferried speedily in Land-Rovers from remote parts of the estate, many hosts prefer to bring their guests into the dry and warm—perhaps a converted stable block or the conservatory if not the actual dining-room. In cases where food is taken to the guns it is kept hot in thermos flasks or insulated boxes, sometimes even in the old-fashioned hayboxes, lined with straw and padded felt. The food itself is quickly prepared, speedily eaten and simple: thick soup, steak and kidney pie, Irish stew and game casserole—the sort of dishes that would have been fed to the beaters in Edwardian days. Drinking is moderate with beer, wine, Horse's Neck (brandy and ginger ale) and whisky soda, with perhaps just a snifter of brandy or port to round the whole thing off.

Many estates have their own lunch specialities and the discerning gun will know, according to the shoot he is on, how much he should eat for breakfast. Much prized is an invitation from the Duke and Duchess of Roxburgh to their Scottish estates, where a lunch of grouse pâté, cold cutlets of meat, croquettes, fruit cake and Stilton, is served in elegant individual silver boxes, a tradition going back to the Twenties.

Although shooting is the premier sport for winter picnics, it is not by any means the only one. Point-to-points are alive with social entertaining of some sort. The Rugby International is another prime picnicking ground. It is possible to spend more time travelling to and from a match at Twickenham than it is watching, so sustenance is essential.

Fishing is a sport that has attracted ardent picnickers from time immemorial. Again it is often a case of necessity, especially if you are on a river bank, miles from nowhere, but with some care and attention the occasion can be raised high above the popular door-step sandwiches and bags of crisps. The noble Piscator from Walton's *The Compleat Angler* had the right idea: 'Go you to yon sycamore tree [he said to friend Venator], and hide your bottle of drink under the hollow root of it; for . . . in that place we will make a brave breakfast with a piece of powdered beef and a radish or two, that I have in my fish-bag.'

During the summer, sporting picnics ascend to the social whirl of Ascot, Wimbledon and Henley, with Badminton (three-day event) and Goodwood (dressage) in close contention, thanks to Royal patronage. At Ascot there is only one place to picnic—No 1 Car Park, alongside the paddock, and a dainty step from the Royal Enclosure. Go anywhere else (other than the owners' park) and you might as well be on the heath with the gypsies. Most of the food consumed here is dinner-party stuff—fancy salmon, fillet of beef Wellington, and strawberries Romanoff—and is eaten in dinner-party style with endless champagne in crystal glasses, damask table linen and the best silver.

A Good Pea Soup *(serves 6)*

2 oz (50 g) butter	8 oz (225 g) dried peas, pre-soaked
1 onion, chopped	Bouquet garni
1 large carrot, chopped	Freshly ground pepper
1 small swede, chopped	1¾ pt (1 l) bacon stock

Melt the butter and gently fry the chopped onion, carrot and swede until softened. Transfer to a large saucepan and add the drained peas, plus all the remaining ingredients.

Bring to the boil, cover and simmer for about 1½ hours. Remove the bouquet garni and liquidise (or sieve) the soup. Return to the pan, season to taste, and reheat.

Pour into a thermos and serve with Wholemeal Baps (see page 65).

Grouse Pâté *(serves 6)*

2 grouse (including livers)
3 tablespoons brandy
8 oz (225 g) streaky bacon, derinded and chopped
8 oz (225 g) pie pork, finely minced

1 clove garlic, crushed
½ teaspoon salt
Freshly ground black pepper
1 teaspoon thyme
1 egg, beaten

Cut the breast meat from the birds in thin strips and marinate in the brandy. Carve away as much of the remaining grouse meat as you can, and chop it finely along with the grouse livers.

Gently fry the bacon and pork in a non-stick frying pan. When some of the fat has been released, add the chopped grouse and livers, and the garlic. Fry for a few minutes more. Transfer the fried meats to a mixing bowl, add the seasonings, thyme, and the drained brandy. Mix in the beaten egg. Place half the mixture in an earthenware dish, cover with the marinated strips of grouse breast and top with remaining pork and grouse mixture. Cover tightly and put in a shallow pan of hot water. Bake in a moderate oven (350°F, 180°C; Gas Mark 4) for 1½–2 hours.

When cool, press the pâté down firmly with a weight and chill overnight in the refrigerator. Serve straight from the earthenware dish with a green salad and crusty bread.

Salmon Mousse *(serves 6)*

12 oz (350 g) cold salmon, cooked and flaked
¾ pt (400 ml) aspic jelly
2 tablespoons dry sherry
Salt and cayenne pepper

½ pt (250 ml) whipping cream
2 egg whites
Hard-boiled eggs, cucumber or green pepper to decorate

Mash the salmon with a fork, fold in the aspic jelly, sherry and the seasonings. (This can be done in a blender—it will give a much smoother purée, but you tend to lose the flavour of the salmon.) Whip the cream and fold it into the purée. Put in a cool place until almost set.

Beat the egg whites until stiff and fold them into the mousse. Taste and season again if necessary. Transfer to a serving dish or individual

ramekins and leave to set in the refrigerator.
Decorate with egg, drained cucumber or green pepper strips. Serve with brown bread and a cucumber salad.

Shrimp and Mushroom Salad *(serves 6)*

12 oz (350 g) shrimps, cooked and peeled
4 oz (125 g) button mushrooms, sliced
2 sticks celery, finely sliced
3 small boiled potatoes, sliced
½ green pepper, seeded and sliced finely
4 tablespoons vinaigrette dressing
1 lettuce, washed and dried
½ cucumber, sliced and drained
3 hard-boiled eggs, sliced
Mayonnaise, thinned slightly with cream or top of the milk
Pinch of dried sage

Toss shrimps, mushrooms, celery, potatoes and green pepper in vinaigrette dressing. Arrange lettuce leaves to form a bed on a large platter. Make a pattern like the spokes of a wheel with the cucumber and hard-boiled egg slices. Spoon the shrimp mixture between the spokes, and lightly coat each shrimp section with thinned mayonnaise. Dust with sage. Cover the entire dish with clingfilm and keep cool until required.

Partridge aux Choux

An authentic Edwardian shooting party recipe, contributed by the Duchess of Devonshire:

'Cook a red cabbage with some slices of Lyon sausage, three pork sausages and three slices of lean bacon; when the cabbage is partly cooked, remove it into a strainer and drain well; from the saucepan carefully remove the sausages etc, leave a little of the gravy.

When the cabbage is thoroughly drained cut it up and place a layer of it in the saucepan, then a layer of sausage, slices of carrot and a thin slice of bacon. Employ all your ingredients in this manner; add, of course, salt and pepper with the addition of a lump of fresh butter, cover with a buttered paper. See that you have sufficient gravy, it must not be dry.

Whilst all this is simmering, put your partridges in a saucepan with a lump of butter, let them cook slowly, baste them frequently, add a little of the gravy you have taken from the other saucepan; when they are cooked and the cabbage is done, place the cabbage, sausage etc carefully on a dish, place the partridges on top and gravy around it.

I do not recommend this as a pretty dish but it is excellent if carefully prepared and all men like it.'

(With acknowledgement to Lady Veronica Maclean in whose book Diplomatic Dishes *this recipe was first published.)*

Not much luck for the shooting party, judging by the solemn faces at this picnic in 1896
(The Mansell Collection)

Beef Wellington *(serves 6)*

8 oz (225 g) mushrooms, chopped
1 small onion, chopped
1 clove garlic, crushed
1 oz (25 g) butter
1 tablespoon cooking oil
Salt and freshly ground black
   pepper

1 teaspoon fresh parsley,
   chopped
1 teaspoon horseradish sauce
1 egg, beaten
2 lb (900 g) fillet of beef
Large packet of puff pastry
   (1 lb/450 g approx)

Fry mushrooms, onion and garlic gently in the butter and oil until soft. Scoop out into a bowl with a slotted spoon, and add the salt, pepper, parsley and horseradish sauce. Mix well and allow to cool. When cold, stir in ⅔ of the beaten egg. Chill the mixture until it is needed.

   Coat the beef fillet lightly in the remaining fat. Place in a roasting tin and cook in a hot oven (425°F, 220°C; Gas Mark 7) for 10 minutes. Remove from the oven and allow to cool completely.

   Roll out the pastry thinly to an oblong just over three times the width of the fillet and with 3 in (7.5 cm) to spare at either end. Lay the beef in the centre of the pastry, spoon the onion and mushroom mixture on top of the meat and bring the edges of the pastry up like a parcel. Brush the seams with water and seal tightly. Turn the pastry over so that the join is at the bottom, and decorate the top with left-over pastry trimmings. Brush with remaining beaten egg and prick a few holes in the top to allow any steam to escape. Bake in a hot oven (425°F, 220°C; Gas Mark 7) for 15 minutes, reducing the heat to moderate (375°F, 190°C; Gas Mark 5) for a further 15 minutes. Allow to cool and carve into thick slices. Wrap in foil.

Boston Baked Beans *(serves 8)*

2 lb (900 g) dried white haricot
  beans
2 teaspoons dry mustard powder
4 tablespoons black treacle
4 tablespoons dark brown sugar
4 tablespoons tomato purée
4 cloves garlic, crushed

2 onions, peeled and sliced
1 bay leaf
1 ½ lb (675 g) belly of pork
Salt and freshly ground black
  pepper
Water

Soak beans overnight in cold water. Drain, put them in a large saucepan and cover with fresh water. Heat slowly and simmer until the skins burst when you lift the beans out of the water in a teaspoon. Drain beans, reserving their cooking liquid. Measure this and make up to 1 pt (500 ml) with water.
    Blend mustard powder with a little of the measured bean liquid. Add black treacle, sugar, tomato purée and crushed garlic. Put beans in a large flattish casserole and pour the mustard mixture over, then add onions, bay leaf, salt and pepper and remaining liquid. Cut grooves 1 in (2.5 cm) deep across the pork and bury it in the beans so that only the rind is showing. Cover casserole and bake in a very slow oven (250°F, 130°C; Gas Mark ½) for about 6 hours, uncovering the casserole for the final hour to brown the pork. Add more water if needed and stir beans from time to time.
    Slice the pork into bite-sized chunks when casserole is cooked. Keep hot in wide-mouthed vacuum flasks until needed.

Jugged Fowl with Oysters *(serves 6–8)*

2 chickens, about 3 lb (1.4 kg)
  each, trussed
1 dozen oysters (or mussels),
  freshly prepared
2 onions, studded with a few
  cloves
2 sticks celery, chopped
8 oz (225 g) carrots, chopped

Bouquet garni
2 pt (1.25 l) chicken stock
¼ pt (150 ml) double cream
1 tablespoon cornflour
2 egg yolks
Salt and pepper
Pinch of ground mace

Place the trussed chickens in a large earthenware casserole, together with half the oysters the onions, celery, carrots, bouquet garni and chicken stock. (If you do not have such a large container, split the ingredients between two.) Cover tightly with a lid, or with greaseproof paper tied with string. Cook in a moderate oven (350°F, 180°C; Gas Mark 4) for 2 hours or until the chickens are tender.

Lift out the birds, strain and skim the liquid. Remove all the meat from the chickens, discarding bones and skin. Blend the cream, cornflour and egg yolks and add to the cooled cooking liquid. Heat slowly in a saucepan over boiling water until this sauce thickens. Add remaining oysters, salt and pepper to taste, and the mace. Simmer for a few minutes more.

Pour sauce over the chicken, warm through (but do not boil) and pour into a wide-mouthed vacuum flask. Serve with Saffron, Orange and Nut Rice Salad (see page 88).

The Beaters' Treat *(serves 6)*

6 large potatoes	4 oz (125 g) streaky bacon,
6 oz (175 g) Cheddar cheese,	cooked and chopped
grated	3 tablespoons fruity pickle
2 oz (50 g) butter, softened	Salt and pepper to taste

Prick the potatoes all over with a fork and bake in a moderately hot oven (400°F, 200°C; Gas Mark 6) for about 1½ hours or until soft.

Slice the top off each potato and scoop out the inside. Mash with 4 oz (125 g) of the cheese, the butter, bacon and pickle. Season to taste.

Pile filling back into potato shells and sprinkle with remaining cheese. Return to the oven for 10–15 minutes at the same temperature to slightly brown the top.

These potatoes are delicious with salt beef or Gammon Cooked In Cider sandwiches (see page 16), and washed down with real ale. They should be transferred straight from the oven to an earthenware casserole dish which has been previously warmed, and kept hot by any means at your disposal (ie insulated boxes, newspapers, spirit-lamp stoves, car-heater vent etc).

Spiced Apple Turnovers *(serves 4–6)*

8 oz (225 g) cooking apples,	1 dessertspoon marmalade
peeled, cored and chopped	Grated rind of ½ lemon
1 oz (25 g) brown sugar	½ level teaspoon mixed spice
1 tablespoon brandy or rum	
1 oz (25 g) sultanas or raisins	8 oz (225 g) puff pastry
½ oz (15 g) chopped dates	Beaten egg to glaze

Put apple, sugar and brandy or rum into a saucepan and cook gently to a pulp. Cool and add other ingredients for the apple filling. Roll out pastry thinly and cut out circles approximately 5 in (13 cm) in diameter using a saucer or bowl as a guide.

Place a scant tablespoon of apple mixture in the centre of each pastry circle. Damp edges with water and bring top edge of circle to bottom to form a 'turnover'. Seal well and place on a greased baking tray. Brush with beaten egg and bake in a hot oven (400°F, 200°C; Gas Mark 6) for 20 minutes.

Allow to cool, dredge with icing sugar and pack into a rigid plastic container lined with a folded paper napkin.

Strawberries Romanoff *(serves 4)*

1 lb (450 g) fresh strawberries, hulled and washed	Juice of 1 orange
	2 tablespoons Grand Marnier
3 tablespoons caster sugar	½ pt (250 ml) whipping cream

Put the strawberries in a bowl, sprinkle with 2 tablespoons of the sugar, the orange juice and Grand Marnier, and leave in the refrigerator for about 1 hour.

Whip the cream with remaining sugar and fold into the strawberries. Turn into a pretty glass or clear plastic serving dish, cover with clingfilm and keep chilled until needed. Serve with sponge fingers or Scandinavian Rings (see page 29).

Whim-wham: An Edwardian Trifle *(serves 6)*

1 pt (500 ml) double cream	Sponge fingers
2 oz (50 g) caster sugar	6 tablespoons redcurrant jelly
4 fl oz (125 ml) white wine	Lemon slices dipped in caster
Grated rind of 1 lemon	sugar to decorate

Whip the cream with the sugar until just stiff, then carefully blend in the wine and grated lemon rind. Spoon a third of this mixture into six individual serving dishes; top each with sliced sponge fingers and ½ tablespoon of redcurrant jelly. Repeat this layering, finishing with the remaining cream and a slice of lemon. Keep well chilled until required, then pack serving dishes into rigid plastic containers.

Huntsman's Ale Cake

1 lb (450 g) mixed fruit	4 oz (125 g) self-raising flour
½ pt (250 ml) brown ale	1 level teaspoon bicarbonate of
8 oz (225 g) butter	soda
8 oz (225 g) soft brown sugar	2 level teaspoons mixed spice
3 eggs	4 oz (125 g) walnuts or almonds,
12 oz (350 g) plain flour	roughly chopped

Steep the fruit in the ale for at least 1 hour, preferably longer, and drain. Cream the butter and sugar until light and fluffy, whisk the eggs with half the drained ale, and beat into butter and sugar mixture.

Mix in the sifted flours, bicarbonate of soda and mixed spice. Add the mixed fruit, nuts and more beer if necessary to make a soft dropping consistency. Spoon into a greased and lined 9–10 in (23–25 cm) cake tin. Smooth the top and bake for 2½–3 hours in a very moderate oven (325°F, 160°C; Gas Mark 3).

When cool, prick the base with a skewer and pour in any remaining ale. Wrap the cake in foil and keep for a while. Serve at the end of a day's shoot with hot brandy or rum toddy.

Rumfustian *(serves 6)*

3 egg yolks
1 pt (500 ml) real ale
⅓ bottle gin
½ bottle medium sweet sherry

1 teaspoon cinnamon
Freshly grated nutmeg
Rind of 1 lemon, thinly pared
6 sugar lumps

Whisk the egg yolks. Warm the ale and gin in a large saucepan, add the egg yolks and mix thoroughly. Heat the sherry, cinnamon, nutmeg, lemon peel and sugar in another pan until almost boiling. Pour over the ale and gin. Adjust spices and sugar to taste, and transfer while still hot to thermos flasks. Serve with warm mince pies.

Pino Colada *(serves 4–6)*

4 fl oz (100 ml) Bacardi rum
4 fl oz (100 ml) dark rum
3 tablespoons thick coconut
  cream
1 heaped tablespoon caster sugar

½ pt (250 ml) pineapple juice
Pinch of salt
Fresh pineapple slices to
  decorate

Put all the ingredients into a cocktail shaker or blender and mix thoroughly. Chill in the refrigerator for at least 1 hour.

Cool the inside of a vacuum flask with cold water and ice cubes. Crush some ice and place in the bottom of the flask. Pour over the chilled rum cocktail.

Before serving, shake the thermos very gently to make sure all the flavours are evenly distributed. If possible, serve with a slice of fresh pineapple.

'VARSITY PICNICS

Come high days and holidays, rag days and regattas, the solid gastronomic curtain of student catering is lifted, and, with no expense
spared from whatever remains of the termly grant, a picnic is put together, lectures and tutorials are avoided and the search for a bus
timetable or a driveable car ensues.

Oxford and Cambridge have always led the way when it comes to
'varsity style, in picnics as in all things. In some cases this has been
dictated through necessity, the college kitchens being so antiquated
that a certain amount of 'porte à manger' has been necessary for
survival.

Count Korsetz writing about pre-World War I Oxford describes
how hampers of food were sent up to him from London to augment the
'abominable' food:

> I totted up that during one month we had polished off three dozen large
> croûte of foie gras, and the invoice from Messrs Solomon of Piccadilly
> listed, among its many items, four hundred custard apples, fifty pounds of
> muscat grapes, and a great gross of hot-house nectarines.

The real height of the 'varsity picnicking season is in the summer,
when exams are, for the most part, over. It is then that the various
'varsity clubs come up with their *al fresco* parties, staging anything
from an open-air bottle party, with every conceivable oddity of dress
from pyjamas to no dress at all, to a full-blooded, thoroughly well-
organised picnic in the grand manner.

At Cambridge, the Titus Oates, a comparatively young dining
society, holds an annual June picnic luncheon at one of two local
beauty spots, Wandlebury Down or Byron's Pool. Dress is informally
formal: collar and tie, white trousers and the society blazer (scarlet
with light blue edgings), altogether a colourful spectacle. A minibus
ferries the majority of diners and serves to transport the cutlery, china
and glassware borrowed from High Table.

The food is elegantly traditional: sherry as an aperitif, dressed crab
or pâté, cold roast beef with new potatoes and various salads, and
sherry trifle with fresh raspberries to follow. Wine from the senior college cellars accompanies the meal and Pimm's No 1 cup rounds it all
off.

41

A picnic at Quarry Woods *(Mary Evans Picture Library)*

Picnics of a slightly more boisterous nature are part of the Cambridge rowing calendar, and are held during the so-called Bumps Week in May. (Oxford has its equivalent celebration in Eights Week.) Although other universities may not possess the glamour and traditions of Oxford and Cambridge, they all have their parks, playing fields, and nearby beauty spots which are favourites with student picnickers. One memory does stand out from my university days and that is of cycling full tilt in a blistering east wind to reach my flat, and seeing clusters of Asian families picnicking in the University Park, seemingly oblivious of the gale that was blowing round their ankles. And they say the English are a stoical race of picnickers! I wish now I had stopped to find out what they were eating.

Herbed Mushroom and Madeira Soup *(serves 6–8)*

2 oz (50 g) butter
8 oz (225 g) onions, chopped
1 clove garlic, crushed
1 lb (450 g) mushrooms, sliced
1 teaspoon dried basil
1 teaspoon dried oregano
½ teaspoon dried thyme

Dash of cayenne pepper
3 fl oz (75 ml) Madeira or sherry
1½ pt (850 ml) chicken stock
2 egg yolks
½ pt (250 ml) single cream
Crisp bacon pieces to garnish

Melt the butter in a large, heavy saucepan. Fry the onions and garlic together gently until soft and transparent. Add the sliced mushrooms and fry for a minute or two more. Add the herbs, seasonings, Madeira or sherry and chicken stock. Bring to the boil, cover and simmer over a low heat for about 1 hour.

Sieve the soup mixture. Beat the egg yolks together with the cream and blend carefully into the soup. Mix well and heat gently (taking care not to boil) prior to pouring into a pre-warmed, large vacuum flask or jug. Serve the soup hot with a sprinkling of crisp bacon added at the last minute before serving.

Prawns in Aïoli *(serves 4)*

1 lb (450 g) fresh cooked prawns	*To garnish:*
White pepper	Cos lettuce
3–4 cloves garlic, crushed	Fresh parsley
2 egg yolks	Lemon slices
Salt and pepper	
½ pt (250 ml) olive oil	

Pick over the prawns to remove heads, legs, tails and scaly bits. Dust with white pepper, drain on kitchen paper and place in a lidded plastic bowl. Put the garlic in a blender, add egg yolks and seasoning and mix for a minute or two. Gradually add the olive oil, drip by drip. (Most blenders have a small hole in the lid for this purpose; if not, cover with tin foil and make a small hole through which you can blend in the oil.)

Continue blending until the garlic mayonnaise (aïoli) is thick and smooth. Add a sufficient quantity to the prawns to suit your taste. Cover and keep chilled.

Take leaves of cos lettuce and sprigs of parsley separately in a plastic bag, plus lemon slices in a twist of clingfilm.

Guacamole *(serves up to 6)*

2 ripe avocados	A few black olives. stoned and
1 clove garlic, crushed	chopped
2 tablespoons lemon juice	A dash of Tabasco sauce
1 tablespoon finely chopped	½ teaspoon chilli powder
onion	2 tablespoons sour cream
2 medium tomatoes. skinned,	Salt and freshly ground black
seeded and chopped	pepper

Remove the flesh from the avocados, scraping the skins thoroughly, and put in a blender with all the other ingredients. Mix well. Adjust the seasoning to suit your taste. Spoon into a plastic container—a large yoghurt carton is ideal—and keep covered. Chill for at least 2 hours.

Houmous *(serves 6–8)*

1 x 15 oz (450 g) can chick peas
2 cloves of garlic, crushed
4 fl oz (100 ml) olive oil
2 tablespoons lemon juice
1/2 level teaspoon ground
coriander
1/2 level teaspoon ground cumin
Dash of cayenne pepper
Salt and freshly ground black
pepper
Chopped mint or parsley to
garnish

Drain the chick peas and put them into a blender together with the garlic, oil, lemon juice, spices and seasonings. Liquidise until the mixture resembles a thick cream.

Transfer houmous to a lidded plastic container, top with chopped mint or parsley and chill until required. Serve with pitta or French bread.

Crab in Curry Mayonnaise *(serves 4 as a main course, 6 as a starter)*

1 lb (450 g) crab meat
1 medium onion, chopped
1 tablespoon cooking oil
2 teaspoons curry powder
1 dessertspoon tomato purée
1 tablespoon thin honey
3 fl oz (75 ml) red wine
2 fl oz (50 ml) water
Juice of 1/2 lemon
Salt and pepper
1/2 pt (250 ml) mayonnaise
Paprika pepper and lettuce to
garnish

Pick over the crab meat carefully to remove any fragments of shell or sinew. Fry the onion gently in oil until soft and transparent; add the curry powder and cook for a few minutes more so that the flavours are absorbed.

Add the tomato purée, honey, wine, water, lemon juice and seasoning and simmer gently until the sauce becomes syrupy.

Allow the sauce to cool, then blend into the mayonnaise and stir in the crab meat. Pile into the centre of a dish lined with lettuce leaves, sprinkle with paprika and serve with a cucumber and tomato salad.

Veal and Watercress Hotpot *(serves 4–6)*

2 medium-sized onions, sliced
1 oz (25 g) butter
1 tablespoon cooking oil
1 1/2 lb (700 g) lean braising veal,
diced
Salt and freshly ground black
pepper
Dried oregano
4 oz (125 g) butter beans,
pre-soaked
1 1/4 pt (675 ml) light stock
Bunch of watercress, chopped
2 tablespoons single cream
2 tablespoons plain yoghurt

Fry the onions gently in the butter and oil until soft; remove from pan and drain on kitchen paper. Fry the veal for about 5 minutes and season well with salt, pepper and a generous pinch of oregano. Add the flour and cook for a minute or two longer, stirring so that the meat is evenly coated.

Place onions and meat in a casserole dish together with pre-soaked beans. Pour stock into the frying pan with the remains of the flour and meat juices. Bring to the boil, stirring continuously, and pour over the meat. Bake in a moderate oven (350°F, 180°C; Gas Mark 4) for 1½ hours.

Add watercress and cook for a further 15 minutes. Blend in yoghurt and cream.

This dish can be cooled and reheated if wished. Keep cold in the refrigerator overnight. On the morning of the picnic, reheat to almost boiling point and pour into a wide-mouthed vacuum flask.

Steak in Sour Cream with Mustard Rice *(serves 4)*

4 thin minute steaks
1 glass of red wine
1 'ablespoon wine vinegar
Juice of ½ orange and thin strips of orange peel
1 teaspoon Worcestershire sauce
Salt and freshly ground black pepper
1 large Spanish onion, sliced
8 oz (225 g) button mushrooms, sliced
Squeeze of lemon juice
¼ pt (150 ml) sour cream

To garnish:
Stuffed olives
Lemon quarters

For the Mustard Rice:
1 cup Patna rice
2 cups chicken stock
⅓ cup salad oil
1 dessertspoon wine vinegar
1 tablespoon French mustard
Salt and ground black pepper

To garnish:
Fresh parsley, chopped

Marinate the steaks overnight in the red wine, vinegar, orange juice and peel, Worcestershire sauce and seasoning. Blanch the onion, boiling gently for about 5 minutes. Stew the mushrooms for about the same length of time in the lemon juice and a little water. Drain and allow to cool.

Drain the steaks and fry very quickly in a little hot oil (about half a minute either side should be adequate if you do not like well-done steak). Drain and cut into thin strips.

Place the meat in a bowl, season with more salt and freshly ground black pepper and add the mushrooms and onions. Stir in the sour cream and adjust the seasoning to taste. Garnish with halved stuffed olives and lemon quarters.

To prepare the Mustard Rice, bring the rice to the boil in the chicken stock, reduce the heat to a gentle simmer, cover tightly and cook for about 8–10 minutes or until the rice is just tender.

Meanwhile, prepare the dressing by blending together the oil, vinegar, mustard and salt and pepper. Pour it over the rice while the latter is still hot. Top with chopped parsley.

Both rice and steak salad should be transported to the picnic site in covered dishes and kept chilled until required. Serve with green or tomato salad.

Shoulder of Lamb with Spiced Rice Stuffing *(serves up to 8)*

4 tablespoons cooking oil
1 medium onion, finely chopped
1 clove garlic, crushed
2 oz (50 g) Patna rice
2 oz (50 g) seedless raisins
2 oz (50 g) dried apricots, chopped
1/2 oz (15 g) flaked almonds, chopped
1 tablespoon fresh mint, chopped

1 teaspoon cinnamon
1/2 teaspoon coriander
1/2 teaspoon ginger
Salt and freshly ground black pepper
1/3 pt (175 ml) hot stock or water
1 lean shoulder of lamb, boned and trimmed of fat

To prepare the stuffing, heat the oil in a large, heavy frying pan and gently fry the onion and garlic until soft and transparent. Add the rice, raisins, apricots, almonds, mint, spices and seasoning and cook for a few minutes more. Add the stock or water; cover and simmer gently for 15 minutes or until the rice has absorbed the liquid.

Allow the stuffing to cool slightly, then spread it inside the meat and roll up the joint, tying securely (but not too tightly) with string. Place in a roasting pan and cook in a moderate oven (350°F, 180°C; Gas Mark 4) for 1 1/2–2 hours.

Transfer to a cold plate and allow the joint to cool. Press it down with a weight and leave in the refrigerator overnight. Cut into slices, removing any string, and wrap in foil.

Beansprout and Bacon Salad *(serves 4–6)*

8 oz (225 g) fresh beansprouts
1 large tomato, skinned, seeded and roughly chopped
1/2 green pepper, seeded and chopped
2 oz (50 g) button mushrooms, sliced
Small bunch spring onions, chopped

4 rashers lean bacon, cooked crisp
3 tablespoons olive oil
1 tablespoon wine vinegar
2 teaspoons soy sauce
Pinch of dry mustard
1/2 teaspoon soft brown sugar
Salt and freshly ground black pepper
Fresh parsley to garnish

Mix the beansprouts in a large salad bowl with the tomato, pepper, mushrooms, spring onions and snippets of crisp bacon. Put all the dressing ingredients into a screw-top jar and shake thoroughly. Just before you are about to set out on the picnic, douse the beansprout

46

salad with the dressing and pack into a lidded plastic container. Top with fresh parsley, cover and keep chilled until needed.

Rhubarb and Pernod Crumble *(serves 4–6)*

1 lb (450 g) rhubarb	3 oz (75 g) butter
1 heaped tablespoon soft brown sugar	6 oz (175 g) flour
	3 oz (75 g) brown sugar
2 tablespoons Pernod (or Ouzo)	3 oz (75 g) ginger biscuits

Wash rhubarb; trim and chop into 1 in (2½ cm) chunks. Pile them into a buttered medium-sized ovenproof dish. Sprinkle with the tablespoon of sugar and Pernod.

To make crumble topping, rub butter into flour to resemble breadcrumbs. Add sugar and mix; add crushed ginger biscuits and mix again. Place on top of the rhubarb and bake on a baking sheet in the middle of a moderately hot oven (375°F, 190°C; Gas Mark 5) for about 45 minutes.

Serve cold (or hot if you can arrange it) with whipped cream. When carrying to the picnic site, it is best to protect the top of the crumble with a layer of foil.

Brown Bread Ice Cream with Hot Cherry Sauce *(serves 4–6)*

3 oz (75 g) brown sugar	1 glass red wine
3 oz (75 g) brown breadcrumbs	½ pt (250 ml) water
2 oz (50 g) icing sugar, sieved	1 tablespoon caster sugar (or more to taste)
½ pt (250 ml) double cream	
2 egg whites	1 tablespoon redcurrant jelly
	Few drops of almond essence
For the sauce:	1 teaspoon arrowroot
1 lb (450 g) cherries, stoned	

Mix the sugar and breadcrumbs and caramelise under the grill. Leave to cool, then break up the crumbs with a fork.

Whisk the icing sugar and cream until thick. Whisk the egg whites separately, and fold into the cream, along with the breadcrumbs. Spoon into a shallow tray or lidded container, and put into the freezer. When almost set give the mixture a thorough stir to prevent ice crystals forming. Stir at least twice more during the freezing process.

To make the sauce, stew the cherries in the wine, water, caster sugar, redcurrant jelly and almond essence. Simmer until the fruit is soft and the sauce slightly thicker. Blend the arrowroot with a little cold water and add to the cooking liquid to make it opaque.

Pack the ice cream into a wide-mouthed thermos flask in fairly small spoonfuls to avoid trapping too much air. Pour the hot sauce into another flask and combine on serving.

47

Rum and Blackcurrant Compote *(serves 4)*

1 lb (450 g) blackcurrants
1 orange
4 oz (125 g) caster sugar
2 level teaspoons arrowroot

1 tablespoon rum
¼ pt (150 ml) whipped cream
Icing sugar

Wash, top and tail the blackcurrants, reserving a few for garnish. Grate the rind from the orange and squeeze its juice. Add water to the juice to make it up to 1 pt (500 ml). Heat the liquid with the sugar in a saucepan until the sugar has dissolved. Bring to the boil and continue boiling for 5 minutes until the syrup has been reduced and thickened slightly.

Add the blackcurrants to the pan and reduce the heat to simmer until tender (about 10–15 minutes).

Blend the arrowroot and rum, add to the blackcurrants and bring syrup to the boil. Cook until clear, then allow to cool.

Spoon into 4 individual serving bowls. Top with whipped cream and the remaining blackcurrants. Dust with a little icing sugar, if possible just before serving. Keep cool and cover with clingfilm or greaseproof paper until required.

Summer Fruit Cake

6 oz (175 g) butter
6 oz (175 g) caster sugar
3 eggs
9 oz (250 g) flour, half plain and
  half self-raising
2 oz (50 g) glacé cherries, halved

8 oz (225 g) mixed dried fruit
Grated rind of ½ lemon
2 tablespoons lemon juice
1 level tablespoon granulated
  sugar

Cream the butter and sugar together until light and fluffy. Beat in the eggs one at a time. In a separate bowl, mix flour, cherries and mixed dried fruit. Fold into the creamed mixture along with lemon rind and juice.

Grease and line a 7 in (18 cm) round cake tin and pile in the mixture. Make sure it is distributed evenly with no air bubbles and level the surface. Sprinkle granulated sugar on top and bake in the middle of a fairly moderate oven (325°F, 160°C; Gas Mark 3) for 1¾ hours until firm or until a skewer inserted into the centre of the cake comes out clean. Wrap in foil, previously sliced if you wish.

Minty Lemon Tea *(serves 4)*

½ lemon
6 sprigs fresh mint
1 dessertspoon sugar

A potful of weak tea
Mint leaves and lemon slices to
  decorate

Pare the lemon rind and put in the teapot along with the fresh mint, sugar and preferred quantity of tea. (If using a mild tea one level teaspoon per person is usually adequate.) Pour on boiling water, stir well and leave to infuse for 10 minutes.

Squeeze juice from ½ lemon and strain into the pot. Stir once and strain tea into a thermos jug. Take along some washed and diced mint leaves and thin lemon slices in a plastic container to serve with each cup of tea.

If desired the tea can be served cold. Strain the tea after the lemon juice has been added and chill. Pour over ice cubes in a thermos jug and serve with mint and lemon as above.

Pimm's No 1

For each drink you will need:

Crushed ice
2 fl oz (50 ml) Pimm's No 1
   mix
¼ pt (150 ml) lemonade

Slice of orange, lemon, a
   Maraschino cherry, cucumber
   chunk and a sprig of mint to
   decorate

Put plenty of crushed ice in the bottom of a ½ pt (250 ml) beer mug. Pour over the Pimm's mix, then the lemonade, and stir. Spike the orange, lemon, Maraschino cherry and cucumber chunk on a cocktail stick and rest across the top of the mug. Finally, garnish with the tip of a mint sprig.

Using the above quantities, allow 1 bottle of Pimm's for 6 people, giving 2 drinks per head. You will find that the first will be downed like fruit squash; the second will prove what a powerful drink it is.

Oxford Punch *(serves up to 8)*

½ pt (250 ml) rum
⅓ pt (175 ml) brandy
3 fl oz (75 ml) lemon squash

1 pt (500 ml) boiling water
Sugar to taste

Mix the rum, brandy and lemon squash in a large thermos flask or jug that will hold at least 2 pt (1.25 l). Pour in the boiling water and add sugar to taste.

LOVERS' PICNICS

It is scarcely surprising that for centuries the picnic has been regarded as the perfect situation for love-making. Where else but in the open air could soul-mates, rich and poor, escape the rigid rules of convention in the one case and the depressing work-a-day existence of the other?

The month of May has always been acknowledged as the month for lovers. Looking back to the days when England had an economy based largely on agriculture, May Day was the signal for spontaneous rejoicing for the crops that were growing in the fields, the young lambs in the meadows and the young leaves on the trees. What could be more natural than that country folk should also celebrate their own fecundity? Thus the natural art of coupling became enshrined in a national May Day custom, with all the attendant garlands, parades and maypole dancing, the Morris Men and mumming plays. Maytime picnics were an essential part of the performance, particularly in the days of Elizabeth I when they were evidently carefully planned and very expensive.

Times have changed, but all hope for Maytime lovers is not lost, for today we enjoy more freedom to come and go and picnic with whom we please, so more cosy intimate lovers' picnics have replaced those enormous communal affairs. Certainly there is no reason to suggest that picnic romances are dead. The present Bishop of Southwark has revealed that he fell in love during one picnic and proposed during another, 'the latter being particularly memorable for the fact that we were sitting on an ant heap at the time'.

The choice of location for a lovers' picnic was believed to be the prime consideration. In Anthony Trollope's *Can You Forgive Her?*, published in 1864, the author clearly does not think much of the beach site chosen for the match-making picnic between the widowed Mrs Greenhow and her two suitors, Mr Cheeseacre and Captain Bellfield. 'There should be trees, broken ground, small paths, thickets, and hidden recesses. There should, if possible, be rocks, old timber, moss and brambles. There should certainly be hills and dales—on a small scale, and, above all, there should be running water. There should be no expanse.'

For advice on the suitability of picnic foods as an aid to 'l'amour' we need look no further than Barbara Cartland, the twentieth-century queen of romantic fiction writers, who also happens to have written

Young couples picnicking *(Museum of English Rural Life, University of Reading)*

two books entitled *Recipes For Love* and *Food for Love*. 'Of course, my dear, you must have plenty of protein to make love', she says. 'Meat has been the acknowledged virility food since the beginning of time: Athenaeus remarks on the large quantity of meat consumed by the Greek captains during the seige of Troy; Horace, the Roman poet, believed in the meat of hares, wild boars and sea urchins; the Chinese have always valued the sex stimulus of duck. But never ever, ever should you take sandwiches. They are very bad for you because you should never mix protein and carbohydrate in that way if you want to stay slim and virile. Instead wrap slices of meat in lettuce; if vegetarian, take something made of soya flour, that is high in protein, and plenty of honey.'

On picnic style she advises: 'Keep things simple, delicate and tasty. Prepare the dishes beforehand, make them look pretty, use attractive disposable plates, cutlery and napkins. There is nothing so unromantic as packing away dirty dishes and shovelling all the scraps into bits of newspaper.'

When you are preparing a picnic for your loved one, or your intended loved one, think in terms of nibbles rather than noshes. An abundance of small, carefully chosen items is vastly preferable to one enormous quiche or joint, and perhaps add some accompanying tit-bits such as fresh peaches, nuts and raisins, marrons glacés, peppermint creams and exquisite chocolates. And don't forget an umbrella; a large golfing one for preference. Many a romance has been signed, sealed and delivered in wet weather.

51

Carrot and Coriander Soup *(serves up to 4)*

1 oz (25 g) butter	2 tablespoons dry sherry
1 small onion, chopped	Salt and freshly ground black
8 oz (225 g) carrots, peeled/	pepper
scraped and chopped	¾ pt (400 ml) chicken stock
½ tablespoon dried coriander	4 tablespoons single cream
1 teaspoon caster sugar	Chopped parsley to garnish

Melt the butter in a large saucepan and gently fry the onion until soft and golden. Add the carrots, coriander, sugar and sherry; season with salt and pepper. Cover and simmer for about 1 hour.

Add the stock and allow to cool slightly. Sieve or liquidise the soup and return to the pan. Reheat and add the cream. When hot (but not boiling) pour into a thermos flask. Carry some chopped, fresh parsley in a yoghurt pot or twist of clingfilm to use as a garnish.

Smoked Salmon Pâté *(serves up to 6)*

3 oz (75 g) soft cream cheese	5 tablespoons double cream
1 tablespoon dry sherry	Paprika
1 tablespoon lemon juice	Lemon or cucumber to decorate
8 oz (225 g) smoked salmon pieces	

Put the cream cheese, sherry, lemon juice and smoked salmon into a blender and liquidise. (Make sure that the cheese is really soft and not just out of the refrigerator.)

Add the cream and a dash of paprika. Scoop the mixture into a small soufflé dish, level the top and decorate with thin slices of lemon or cucumber. Chill overnight.

On the morning of the picnic, cover with clingfilm and keep as cool as possible (ideally in an ice box) until required. Serve with buttered rye or granary bread.

Stuffed Figs in Parma Ham *(serves 2)*

4 fresh figs	Pinch of cayenne pepper
2 oz (50 g) soft cream cheese	2 oz (50 g) Parma ham, in 4 thin
1 tablespoon mayonnaise	slices
Salt and ground black pepper	

Split each fig almost in two, from top to bottom. Blend the cream cheese with the mayonnaise and season to taste with salt, pepper and cayenne. Divide the cheese mixture into four and spoon a quarter into each fig. Wind a slice of Parma ham around one of the figs and secure with a cocktail stick. Repeat with the other three.

If you can get hold of fig leaves, wash and dry one or two and use to line the plate on which the figs are served.

Spiced Chicken *(serves up to 6)*

3 oz (75 g) butter
Large pinch of ground ginger
¼ teaspoon cinnamon
Large pinch of cayenne pepper
Lemon juice

Garlic salt
Freshly ground black pepper
6 boned chicken breasts
Lettuce, watercress and radishes
   to garnish

Cream the butter with a fork: add the spices and lemon juice and season with garlic salt and black pepper.

Remove the skin from the chicken and dry the meat carefully. Coat generously with the spicy butter and cook under a medium hot grill for about 20 minutes, turning once and basting frequently.

When cold, lay the chicken on a platter covered with lettuce leaves, garnish with watercress and radishes sliced into fan shapes.

Midsummer Duck *(serves up to 4)*

1 duckling, about 4 lb (1.8 kg)
Salt and pepper
2 oranges
2 sticks tender celery, finely
   chopped
1 tablespoon walnuts, chopped
4 fl oz (100 ml) dry white wine
1 tablespoon lemon juice
2 teaspoons onion, finely chopped
1 teaspoon onion salt

1 teaspoon fresh tarragon, finely
   chopped

Sour Cream dressing:
3 oz (75 g) full cream cheese
¼ pt (150 ml) sour cream
3 drops Tabasco sauce
½ teaspoon caster sugar
Salt and freshly ground black
   pepper

Wash and dry the duck thoroughly, inside and out. Prick all over and rub salt into the skin; season the inside of the bird with salt and pepper, and stuff with the pared rind of the oranges. Place on a rack in a roasting tin with about ¼ in (5 mm) of water in the bottom. Roast uncovered in a moderate oven (350°F, 180°C; Gas Mark 4) for about 1½ hours, basting occasionally. Allow to cool.

Remove the pith from the oranges, separate the segments and slice each segment in half. Put into a bowl with the celery and walnuts and set aside.

To prepare the marinade, mix together the wine, lemon juice, onion, salt and tarragon. Slice all the meat from the cooled duck, discarding bones and skin. Put meat and marinade in a shallow dish, cover and refrigerate for 12–18 hours, turning the meat once or twice.

To prepare the sour cream dressing, put the cheese, sour cream, Tabasco sauce and sugar into a blender and mix thoroughly. Season to taste with pepper and salt.

Drain the marinade from the duck. Mix the meat with the oranges, celery and walnuts. Line a plate with lettuce leaves, pile the salad on top and garnish with watercress sprigs. Cover with clingfilm. Keep the dressing separate in a small plastic bowl, and pour over the duck just before serving.

Chilly Day Beef *(serves up to 4)*

1–1½ lb (500–675 g) stewing steak
1 tablespoon seasoned flour
8 oz (225 g) onions, chopped
1 clove garlic, crushed
1 oz (25 g) cooking fat
4 oz (125 g) button mushrooms, sliced

1 x 15 oz (450 g) can tomatoes, roughly chopped
2 rounded teaspoons English mustard
1 heaped tablespoon sweet pickle
1 heaped tablespoon thin honey
2 level teaspoons paprika

Trim the meat and cut into cubes. Toss in the seasoned flour. Fry the onions and garlic gently in the fat until soft and transparent. Drain and set aside.

Turn up the heat and brown the meat on all sides. Add the sliced mushrooms and cook together for a few moments. Transfer meat, onions and mushrooms to a casserole.

Pour the canned tomatoes into the frying pan and bring to the boil, stirring all the time to incorporate all the pan juices. Remove from the heat, add the remaining ingredients, mix thoroughly and pour into the casserole.

Cover the dish tightly and cook in a very moderate oven (325°F, 160°C; Gas Mark 3) for 2½–3 hours until the meat is really tender.

Pour into a wide-mouthed flask and serve with fresh crusty bread.

Cottage Cheese Luncheon Rollers *(serves up to 4)*

8 large lettuce leaves
Salt and pepper
6 oz (175 g) cottage cheese
2 oz (50 g) Cheddar cheese, grated

2 spring onions, finely chopped
1 oz (25 g) walnuts, chopped
1 tablespoon soy sauce
Dash of paprika

Wash the lettuce leaves and pat dry carefully. Lay them out flat and season lightly with salt and pepper. Combine the cheeses, onion, nuts, soy sauce and paprika. Season to taste.

Place a spoonful of this mixture on each lettuce leaf, roll up and secure with cocktail sticks. Keep well chilled in a plastic container. Serve with a herby tomato salad and wholemeal bread.

Spinach Puffs *(makes 8 puffs)*

8 oz (225 g) fresh spinach
2 oz (50 g) cottage cheese, sieved
1 egg, beaten

1 tablespoon Parmesan cheese, grated
Squeeze of lemon juice

Salt and freshly ground black
    pepper
8 oz (225 g) puff pastry

2 oz (50 g) Swiss cheese, finely
    sliced
2 slices of ham, quartered
Beaten egg to glaze

Cook the spinach until just tender. Drain thoroughly and chop finely.
Combine with the sieved cottage cheese, beaten egg and Parmesan
cheese. Add a squeeze of lemon juice, salt and freshly ground black
pepper, and mix thoroughly.
    Roll out the pastry thinly and cut into oblongs approximately 5 x 3
in (13 x 8 cm). Put a dessertspoonful of spinach mixture on one half of
each oblong, top with some sliced Swiss cheese and a quarter of ham.
Damp the edges of the pastry, fold up the puff and seal carefully.
Make a slit in the top of each puff for the steam to escape and brush
with beaten egg. Bake in a hot oven (400°F, 200°C; Gas Mark 6) for
15–20 minutes. Cool: pack into a tin or rigid plastic container.

Mozzarella-stuffed Tomatoes *(serves up to 4)*

4 large tomatoes
6 rashers streaky bacon, fried
    crisp
2 oz (50 g) Mozzarella cheese,
    thinly sliced
4 spring onions or baby leeks

2 tablespoons sour cream
Salt and freshly ground black
    pepper
1 tablespoon oil
Squeeze of lemon
Parsley to garnish

Cut a thin slice from the top of each tomato. Scoop out the pulp with a
teaspoon. Retain the tomato flesh; discard the juice and pips.
    Roughly chop the bacon, cheese, onions and tomato. Put in a bowl
and cover with a sauce made from the sour cream, salt and pepper, oil
and lemon.
    Pile the salad back into the tomato cups, garnish with chopped
parsley and chill until required. Carry to the picnic site in either a
light casserole dish or bowl covered with clingfilm, or a rigid plastic
box (an ice-cream container is practical if not beautiful).

Fresh Fruit with Honey Yoghurt *(serves 2)*

1 small carton natural yoghurt
1 generous tablespoon thin
    honey
Squeeze of lemon juice
A little grated lemon rind
Drop of vanilla essence

Peeled and sliced fresh fruit—
    strawberries, oranges, peaches
    apples, bananas (dipped in
    lemon juice), melon, pears, etc
2 teaspoons wheatgerm or
    chopped nuts

Mix yoghurt, honey, lemon juice, rind and vanilla essence together in
one plastic container. Put prepared fruits in another. Keep well chil-

led until required. Pour the honey yoghurt over the fruit just before serving and top with wheatgerm or chopped nuts (which, of course, you have remembered to take along separately).

Orange Jelly Baskets *(serves 2–3)*

4 large oranges	¼ pt (150 ml) hot water
2½ fl oz (60 ml) medium sherry	4 oz (125 g) caster sugar
1 lemon	Whipped cream to decorate
½ oz (15 g) or 1 envelope gelatine	

Wash the oranges and peel one as thinly as possible. Soak the peel in the sherry for at least 1 hour.

Cut the remaining 3 oranges into basket shapes by removing two large wedge shapes on either side of the upper half and leaving a strip of rind at the top to form the handle. Remove the pulp from all the oranges, add the lemon flesh and liquidise. Strain juice into a jug.

Dissolve gelatine in the water. (It is easiest to do this in a cup, standing it in a pan of hot water.) Tip the water out of the pan, add the sugar and dissolved gelatine, and heat gently, stirring regularly, until the sugar has also dissolved. Add the orange and lemon juice, and the sherry, strained to remove the peel.

Pour into the orange peel baskets and leave overnight to set. Decorate with whipped cream. To be truly romantic, serve on a leaf plate with Chocolate Almond Biscuits (below).

Peach Syllabub *(serves 2–3)*

4 tablespoons dry white wine	2–3 ripe peaches, skinned,
1 tablespoon caster sugar	stoned and sliced
1 tablespoon lemon juice	¼ pt (150 ml) double cream
A little grated lemon rind	Flaked almonds to decorate
Drop of almond essence	

Put the wine, sugar, lemon juice, rind and almond essence in a bowl. Add the peaches and leave for several hours.

Whip the cream until stiff. Drain the peaches and spoon the slices into 2 or 3 individual serving dishes. Combine the juice with the cream and spread the mixture on top of the peaches. Sprinkle flaked almonds on top, cover with clingfilm and keep icy cold until required.

Chocolate Almond Biscuits *(makes about 20 biscuits)*

2 egg whites	1 oz (25 g) blanched almonds,
2 oz (50 g) icing sugar	finely chopped
2 oz (50 g) ground almonds	2 oz (50 g) plain chocolate

Whisk the egg whites until stiff but not dry. Whisk in half the sugar.

Fold in the remaining sugar and ground almonds. Line 2 baking sheets with greased greaseproof paper and spoon out the mixture into circles, about 2½ in (6 cm) in diameter. Sprinkle with chopped almonds.

Bake in the centre of a very slow oven (225°F, 110°C; Gas Mark ¼) for 25–30 minutes. The biscuits should be firm but not crisped or browned. Curve the biscuits slightly round a rolling pin.

Melt the chocolate in a dry basin over a saucepan of hot water. Spread the underside of each biscuit with chocolate and leave to harden.

Wholewheat Nut and Banana Bread

4 tablespoons honey
4 oz (125 g) butter
3 ripe bananas, mashed
1 teaspoon vanilla essence
2 eggs, beaten
3 oz (75 g) wholewheat flour

3 oz (75 g) plain flour
2 oz (50 g) wheatgerm
2 teaspoons baking powder
½ teaspoon salt
½ teaspoon cinnamon
3 oz (75 g) chopped nuts

Cream the honey and butter. Stir in the bananas, vanilla essence and beaten eggs. Combine the rest of the ingredients in a separate bowl and mix thoroughly. Fold into the butter and banana mixture. Spoon into a greased loaf tin, approximately 5 x 9 in (13 x 23 cm) and bake in a very moderate oven (325°F, 160°C; Gas Mark 3) for 1–1¼ hours or until the loaf is golden brown.

Allow to cool, slice and spread with farmhouse butter. Sandwich the slices together for ease of carrying and wrap in foil. Separate them when you get to the picnic site.

Turkish Delight *(makes 25–30 pieces)*

8 oz (225 g) granulated sugar
¾ pt (400 ml) water
Pinch cream of tartar
1¾ oz (45 g) cornflour
4 oz (125 g) icing sugar

2 teaspoons rose water
1 oz (25 g) blanched almonds,
    finely chopped
Extra icing sugar and cornflour
    to coat

Dissolve sugar in ¼ pt (150 ml) of water by stirring in a saucepan over moderate heat. Bring to the boil and cook, without stirring, for about 8–10 minutes until a drop of the sugar mixture reaches soft ball stage. (To test for this, place a drop of the mixture into cold water. If rolled with the fingers it should form a soft ball.) Sprinkle on the cream of tartar.

While syrup is cooking, mix cornflour and icing sugar with 4 tablespoons of the water to form a smooth paste. Top up the remaining water to ½ pt (250 ml) and put on to heat in another saucepan. When hot, stir in the cornflour and icing sugar and boil for 3 minutes, stirring continuously. Add syrup gradually to the cooked cornflour mixture, beating well, and boil for 10 minutes, stirring continuously. By now your mixture should be pale golden colour and almost clear.

Finally, stir in the rose water and chopped almonds and pour into a greased flat tin, approximately 6 in ((15 cm) square. Leave to set. Line a pretty sweet or chocolate box with greaseproof paper. Cut the Turkish Delight into squares, coat with a sieved mixture of 1 tablespoon icing sugar to ½ tablespoon cornflour and pack into the box, sprinkling any remaining sugar mixture between each layer.

Loving Cup *(serves up to 4)*

1 lemon	¾ pt (400 ml) crushed ice
2 oz (50 g) lump sugar	¼ pt (150 ml) brandy, Madeira
1 orange	or sherry
Lemon balm	½ bottle champagne or dry
Borage	sparkling white wine

Rub the peel of the lemon with sugar lumps. Slice the peel finely, remove the pith, and thinly slice the lemon flesh. Halve the orange. Pare the rind and slice the flesh of one half; squeeze the juice from the other.

Put the sliced lemon and peel, and the sliced orange, juice and peel in a bowl with a couple of sprigs of lemon balm and borage, the sugar lumps and the crushed ice. Leave for about 4 hours in the refrigerator.

Stir in the alcohol, drain and pour into a large vacuum flask or, preferably, a vacuum jug. Carry the ½ bottle of champagne (well chilled) to the picnic and pour into the flask or jug just before serving. Retain a few lemon and orange slices in a small plastic container to float on the surface of the Loving Cup as an innocent diversion.

Passion Punch *(serves 2–4)*

1 orange	4 tablespoons icing sugar
1 lemon	1 pt (500 ml) dry ginger ale
1 peach	Ice cubes
4 oz (125 g) strawberries, hulled	Fresh mint leaves to decorate

Remove the peel and pith from the orange and lemon, divide into segments and extract the pips. Peel the peach, remove the stone and cut into slices.

Put the prepared orange, lemon and peach flesh into a blender, along with the hulled strawberries and the sugar. Add a little ginger ale and mix thoroughly. Strain the fruit through a fine sieve and combine in a large jug with the ginger ale.

Pour into a thermos flask half-filled with ice cubes. Serve decorated with a few fresh mint leaves.

THE WORKINGMAN'S PICNIC

There is a widely held belief—spread abroad by popular novels, TV series, and books and products with a 'country kitchen' theme—that the workingman of yesteryear lived and fared better than his counterpart today. In one respect only could this be said to be true—if he was out in the open air, he was probably fitter than the present-day factory worker who spends all day at a production line and all evening gazing at the goggle box.

Whether he was actually healthier is another matter. The diet of the agricultural labourer until the beginning of this century was, for the most part, meagre and low in certain vitamins. As far back as the Middle Ages, bread and cheese, curds and cream were the regular stand-bys, eggs and bacon the irregular luxuries. The usual practice was for labourers to have their main meal at midday, and as this would be eaten in the fields where they were working to avoid spending time on the long trek home, it was, perforce, a picnic. A chunk of bread, some cheese, onions for flavour, and ale would have been a typical dinner for the medieval worker; a bill of fare alleviated by the occasional salt herring to mark fish days, which were ordained by the church on the grounds that fish eating was thought to reduce carnal passions.

The partnership of bread and cheese is such a cornerstone of the workingman's diet that it is hardly surprising the two are imbedded in so many customs and curiosities. In some parts of the country cheeses were (and still are) given to symbolise good luck, particularly at the birth of a baby. In Cheshire, right up until the late nineteenth century, farmers paid their rent in cheese, while during the Peasants' Revolt in 1381, anybody who said 'bread and cheese' with a foreign accent went to the block.

Although the partnership of bread and cheese has been institutionalised into the Ploughman's Lunch, it was not a ploughman who first thought up the name. Surprisingly the name is of recent introduction. According to the English Country Cheese Council, their former chairman, gentleman-farmer Sir Richard Trehane, marched into a Surrey pub in 1954 and demanded a plate of crusty bread and cheese, a lunch 'fit for a ploughman', which he palpably was not. Nevertheless the term stuck and now pubs from John O'Groats to Land's End serve the venerable 'ploughman's' to workers of every description (often with a type of cheese that would give Sir Richard hiccups).

The cottage-kept pig provided cold bacon or lard to eat with the bread, or perhaps a slice of bacon suet pudding. In some parts of the country the pastry would enclose both savoury and sweet fillings, giving two courses in one pie or 'clanger', surely the first convenience food. This meal, eaten on the dot of noon became known as 'noonshun' and subsequently 'nuncheon', from which we derive luncheon. In Jane Austen's *Sense and Sensibility* the word nuncheon is used to suggest a rough and hasty meal such as might be consumed by an impatient horseman while his horse is being rubbed down at the inn. 'Bever' was another expression commonly used for the midday meal taken in haste.

The following description is of a grim sort of picnic, but a picnic it usually was, eaten in whatever fresh air was available. A Staffordshire potter's boy recalls of the 1840s: 'Bread and butter was made up in a handkerchief, with a sprinkling of tea and sugar. Sometimes there was a little potato pie with a few pieces of fat bacon on it.' Baked or boiled potatoes were regular working lunches, so too were pies or pasties—if the workers could afford them—bought from a street trader at a penny a time.

The shape of these pies varied greatly from one part of the country to another, and would sometimes contain literally anything the wily housewives could lay their hands on. Few people today will have heard of the Lancashire Foote, the Checky Pig or the Banbury, Clifton

'Crust time' at the Dalcoath mines, 1906 (*John Topham Picture Library*)

or Coventry type of folding for pastry, but most are familiar with the Cornish pasty, which some say is elliptical in shape because it was easier to throw down the mines to the workers below. (Another far more plausible theory is that the pastry was joined at the top to avoid spilling gravy in the old Cornish hearth ovens.)

All this seems a long way from the kind of lunch break which office and factory workers have today. And yet, with the trend moving towards automatic vending machines, there is a strong case in favour of the picnic lunch, be it on a desk top, town park-bench or factory lawn. In many towns and cities, sandwich shops and hamburger bars are moving in to fill this need, but how much tastier is a home-packed hunk of crusty freshly baked bread with farmhouse cheese or pâté, than a slab of flattened mince between starchy buns or a glutinous milk shake of bath salts hue?

Fresh Tomato and Lentil Soup *(serves 6)*

1 medium-sized onion, peeled and sliced	1 1/2 pt (850 ml) chicken stock
1 medium-sized potato, peeled and sliced	1 lb (450 g) ripe tomatoes, peeled and sieved
2 oz (50 g) butter	2 teaspoons celery salt
4 oz (125 g) lentils	Freshly ground black pepper
	1 teaspoon sugar

Chop the onion and potato and fry gently in a large saucepan with butter for 5 minutes. Grind lentils in a liquidiser for 2 minutes. Add stock and ground lentils to pan. Stir well. Cover and simmer for about 1 hour, stirring from time to time.

Add sieved tomatoes, seasoning and sugar, and simmer for a further 10 minutes.

Liquidise when cool. Reheat when needed and pour into a pre-warmed vacuum flask.

Potted Cheese *(serves 4–6)*

3 oz (75 g) unsalted butter	1 tablespoon chopped chives
8 oz (225 g) Cheshire cheese, finely grated	Pinch of cayenne pepper
2 tablespoons port	Chopped chives or pickled walnut to garnish
Dash of Worcestershire sauce	

Cream the butter and gradually beat in the grated cheese. Stir in the port, Worcestershire sauce, chives and cayenne pepper and mix thoroughly.

Spoon into 1 large or 4–6 individual pots and chill. Garnish with more chopped chives or a pickled walnut. Cover with clingfilm and keep cool, preferably in an insulated box.

Beer and Rabbit Pâté *(serves up to 8)*

2 lb (900 g) rabbit, boned and
    chopped
½ pt (250 ml) light ale
1 lb (450 g) belly of pork, skinned
    and chopped

2 cloves garlic, crushed
1 teaspoon dried thyme
Salt and ground black pepper
2 bay leaves
6 oz (175 g) streaky bacon

Marinate all the ingredients except the bacon rashers in a covered bowl overnight, then mince the pork and rabbit separately.

Remove the bacon rinds and stretch the rashers with the blade of a knife. Use them to line a 1 lb (450 g) loaf tin. Pack the meat into the tin in layers. Pour over the drained beer liquid. Cover with foil and bake in a slow oven (300°F, 150°C; Gas Mark 2) for 2½–3 hours.

Remove from the oven and weight down until cold and set firmly. Wrap individual slices in foil, and eat with fresh crusty bread.

Cold Curried Prawns and Eggs *(serves 4)*

4 eggs
2 tablespoons oil
1 tablespoon onion, finely
    chopped
1 clove garlic, crushed
1 level dessertspoon curry powder

1 teaspoon tomato purée
¼ pt (150 ml) water
½ pt (250 ml) Family
    Mayonnaise (see page 89)
8 oz (225 g) prawns, peeled
Sprigs of watercress to garnish

Hard-boil the eggs by simmering for 10 minutes and plunging immediately into cold water. (This prevents the ugly black ring forming around the yolk.)

Put the oil in a heavy frying pan and gently cook the onion and garlic until soft and transparent. Add the curry powder and cook for a few minutes more. Then add the tomato purée and water, and simmer until the liquid is reduced to a thick sauce. Allow to cool slightly and add to the mayonnaise, stirring thoroughly to mix the two.

Cut the hard-boiled eggs in half and place cut side downwards in a rigid plastic container. Sprinkle the prawns around the eggs and pour the sauce on top. Garnish with watercress and keep chilled until required. Serve with a salad of tomato and cucumber and buttered dark rye crispbread.

Cornish Pasties *(serves 6–8)*

12 oz (350 g) self-raising flour
1 teaspoon salt
5 oz (150 g) fat (lard and
    margarine)
2½ fl oz (60 ml) cold water

For the filling:
12 oz (350 g) lean steak (cheap
    rump is ideal, stewing steak
    passable)
1 small onion, chopped

62

6 oz (175 g) potato, peeled and
   diced
1 small turnip, chopped
1 tablespoon dark, fruity pickle
1 dessertspoon water, stock, or

best of all, beef jelly from the
   bottom of the dripping bowl
Salt and freshly ground black
   pepper
Beaten egg to glaze

Sift the flour and salt and rub in the fat until the mixture resembles fine breadcrumbs. Add the water, bind the pastry and leave to chill for 20 minutes.

Cut the trimmed steak into strips about ½ in (13 mm) wide, then cut each strip into slivers with a very sharp knife. Mix the onion, potato, turnip, pickle, stock/jelly and seasoning in a bowl. Add the meat and mix well.

Roll out the pastry thinly and cut into 6 in (15 cm) circles using a saucer as a guide. Spoon some meat mixture into the centre of each round, damp the edges carefully and draw up to form a seam at the top. Pinch firmly between the fingers to make a neat ridge. Seal well.

Place on a baking sheet, brush with beaten egg and bake in a hot oven (425°F, 220°C; Gas Mark 7) for a further 30 minutes to cook the filling.

Cool on a wire rack and when completely cold, pack into a rigid plastic container lined with a folded paper napkin.

Mint-crisped Lamb Cutlets *(serves 3)*

1 lean best end of lamb
Salt and freshly ground black
   pepper
2 tablespoons gooseberry and mint
   jelly (or redcurrant jelly

with a teaspoon of
   concentrated mint sauce)
Paper frills, lettuce and
   watercress to decorate

Ask your butcher to prepare the lamb as for Guards of Honour or Crown Roast (ie chined and cut away to reveal the rib bones).

Wipe the meat over with kitchen paper to dry it thoroughly; season with salt and pepper and place the joint in a roasting tin with the fat side uppermost. Roast in a hot oven (425°F, 220°C; Gas Mark 7) for 40–45 minutes.

Melt the jelly in a small saucepan. Remove meat from the oven 15 minutes before the cooking is complete. Using a pastry brush, spread the melted jelly over the top of the lamb, then return meat to the oven for remainder of cooking time.

Cool meat as quickly as possible and chill in the refrigerator. Chop into individual cutlets when cold, fit each cutlet with a paper frill and place in a plastic box lined with washed and dried lettuce leaves. Garnish with sprigs of watercress, cover with clingfilm and keep cold until required.

Everyman Salad *(serves 2 generously)*

1 small cos lettuce	*For the dressing:*
½ small cauliflower	5 tablespoons olive oil
2 sticks celery	2 tablespoons white wine vinegar
Bunch of watercress leaves	½ teaspoon French mustard
4–6 spring onions	Pinch of caster sugar
2 oz (50 g) mushrooms	Salt and freshly ground black
3 oz (75 g) salami, whole not sliced	pepper
3 oz (75 g) Gruyère cheese	
Fresh parsley, chopped	

Wash the lettuce, dry thoroughly, , and shred it, leaf by leaf, into a large salad bowl. Break the washed cauliflower into florets and slice into bite-size pieces. Prepare the celery and slice finely. Chop the watercress and spring onions; slice the mushrooms. Add all these ingredients to the salad bowl. Slice the salami and cheese into matchstick strips. Toss into the salad bowl along with a sprinkling of fresh chopped parsley and mix thoroughly. Make up the salad dressing in a screw top jar and keep both salad and dressing well chilled. Pile the salad into one or two rigid plastic containers before you set off to work. Take the dressing aiong to pour over the salad at the last minute.

Ambrosia *(serves 2)*

1 banana	2 teaspoons wheatgerm
1 small carton natural yoghurt	1 tablespoon chopped nuts
1 tablespoon thin honey	1 tablespoon grated chocolate

Mash the banana with the yoghurt and honey in a small bowl. Stir in the wheatgerm and divide between 2 small dishes (or clean 5 oz [150 g] yoghurt pots). Top with the chopped nuts and grated chocolate. Cover with clingfilm.

Coffee Baked Custard *(makes 4–6 individual custards)*

3 eggs	Extra caster sugar for sprinkling
2 oz (50 g) caster sugar	Whipped cream and grated
½ pt (250 ml) milk	chocolate to decorate
1½ tablespoons coffee essence	
(or 3 teaspoons instant coffee	
with hot water added)	

Whisk the eggs and sugar together. Bring the milk to just under boiling point, then gradually whisk into the egg mixture. Stir in the coffee essence. Lightly butter 4–6 individual ramekin dishes and sprinkle their sides with caster sugar. Strain the custard into the dishes. Stand them in a roasting tin containing some very hot water, cover with a sheet of greaseproof paper and bake in a moderate oven (325°F, 160°C; Gas Mark 3) for 50–55 minutes or until just set. Remove from oven and roasting tin.

When cold, decorate the custards with whipped cream and grated chocolate, if liked. Cover with clingfilm and keep chilled if possible.

Ported Pears *(serves 4)*

4–6 hard, green pears	Grated rind of 1 lemon, thinly
6 oz (175 g) granulated sugar	pared
1 pt (500 ml) water	4 tablespoons red port

Peel, halve and core the pears. Dissolve the sugar in the water, add the lemon rind and pears and bring to the boil. Reduce the heat and simmer gently until the pears are almost tender. Pour in the port and cook for a few minutes more. Remove the pears from the cooking liquid with a slotted spoon. Strain the liquid into a clean saucepan and reduce over a fierce heat to make a thick syrup. Pour this over the pears and allow to cool.

Spoon a portion of pears and syrup into an individual serving dish or lidded plastic container (an 8 oz [225 g] cottage cheese pot is ideal). Keep in the refrigerator until required.

Oatcakes *(makes 12–14)*

6 oz (175 g) oatmeal	¼ teaspoon bicarbonate of soda
2 oz (50 g) rolled oats	1 oz (25 g) margarine
Pinch of salt	6 tablespoons warm water

Measure the oatmeal, oats, salt and bicarbonate of soda into a mixing bowl and blend thoroughly together. Melt the margarine and add to the oat mixture, together with the warm water, to make a stiff dough. Roll out to ¼ in (6 mm) thick.

Using a medium cutter, score the dough into small rounds. Place on a well-greased baking sheet. Bake in a hot oven (450°F, 230°C; Gas Mark 8) for 10–15 minutes, turning once.

When cool sprinkle with a little dry oatmeal and pack into a rigid plastic container lined with greaseproof paper.

Wholemeal Baps *(makes 15–20)*

1 lb (450 g) wholemeal flour	1 oz (25 g) fresh yeast (or
8 oz (225 g) strong plain flour	4 teaspoons dried yeast and
1 dessertspoon salt	2 teaspoons caster sugar)
1 dessertspoon caster sugar	¾ pt (400 ml) warm water
½ oz (15 g) lard	

Sift the flours and the salt together. Mix in the caster sugar and rub in the lard. Blend the fresh yeast with the water (or dissolve the 2 teaspoons of sugar in the water, sprinkle on the dried yeast and leave for about 10 minutes until frothy).

Add the yeast liquid to the dry ingredients and mix to a soft, elastic dough. (Some wholemeal flours absorb more liquid than others so add extra water if you think it looks too dry.) Turn onto a floured board and knead well until smooth. Shape the dough into a round ball and place in a large, lightly-oiled polythene bag. Tie loosely and leave to rise in a warm place for about 1 hour, until it doubles in size.

When risen, turn the dough onto a floured board and knead again until firm. Divide into 15 or more balls of dough. Flatten each one with the palm of the hand and place on a greased baking sheet. Brush with milk, dust with flour and leave to rise for a further 15–20 minutes. Press down and dust with flour again, and bake in a hot oven (425°F, 220°C; Gas Mark 7) for 15–20 minutes.

Junes' Rhubarb Chutney

4 lb (1.8 kg) rhubarb, sliced	2 tablespoons ground mixed spice
1 lb (450 g) onions, peeled and sliced	2 teaspoons ground ginger
	2 teaspoons curry powder
8 oz (225 g) dates, chopped	2 lb (900 g) sugar
1 pt (500 ml) malt vinegar	1 oz (25 g) salt

Put the rhubarb, onions and dates in a large saucepan and add half the vinegar. Cook slowly over a low heat until tender.

Add the spices, sugar, salt, and the remainder of the vinegar, and stir well. Simmer gently until thick. When slightly cooled, pot in warm, dry jars. Cover and seal.

Lincolnshire Plum Bread

4 oz (125 g) prunes	7 oz (200 g) self-raising flour
4 oz (125 g) butter	Pinch of salt
4 oz (125 g) Demerara sugar	½ teaspoon mixed spice
2 eggs, beaten	¾ teaspoon cinnamon
½ teaspoon liquid gravy browning	4 oz (125 g) currants
1 tablespoon brandy	4 oz (125 g) sultanas

Steep prunes overnight in water to plump them up; remove their stones and chop the fruit finely. Cream the butter and sugar; blend in the beaten eggs, gravy browning and brandy.

Sift the flour into a separate bowl with the salt, mixed spice and cinnamon. Add the currants and sultanas and mix thoroughly.

Gradually fold the dry ingredients into the butter and sugar mixture. Add the chopped prunes and mix well. Spoon the mixture into a greased and lined 2 lb (900 g) loaf tin. Bake in a very slow oven (250°F, 130°C; Gas Mark ½) for 2–2½ hours.

Allow to cool in the tin, then turn out and wrap in foil. This cake improves with keeping and is delicious when cut in slices and spread with farmhouse butter.

Lemon Butter Cake

8 oz (225 g) butter	8 oz (225 g) plain flour
8 oz (225 g) caster sugar	2 level teaspoons baking powder
Finely grated rind and juice of	3 oz (75 g) mixed peel, chopped
1 lemon	6 oz (175 g) granulated sugar
4 eggs	

Beat the butter and sugar until light and creamy. Add the grated lemon rind and beat in the eggs, one at a time.

Sift the flour and baking powder together and add gradually to the butter and sugar mixture. Stir in half the mixed peel.

Spoon the mixture into a lined and greased 7–8 in (18–20 cm) cake tin. Smooth the top and sprinkle with the remaining mixed peel. Bake in a very moderate oven (325°F, 160°C; Gas Mark 3) for 1¾ hours, or until a skewer inserted into the centre of the cake comes out clean.

Mix lemon juice and granulated sugar together. Turn cake out of the tin onto a wire rack. Pour sugar and lemon mixture over the top of the hot cake and leave to cool. Cut a slice for lunch or tea, and wrap in foil.

Citrus Fruit Cup *(serves 4–6)*

4 oz (125 g) caster sugar	2 lemons
¼ pt (150 ml) water	1 grapefruit
4 oranges	1 pt (500 ml) tonic or soda water

Make a sugar syrup by dissolving the sugar in the water. Bring to the boil and simmer for 5–10 minutes. Allow to cool.

Squeeze the juice from the oranges, lemons and grapefruit. Add to the sugar syrup when cool, and leave for a few hours in the refrigerator.

Just before setting off for your working picnic, slide a few chunks of ice into a 2 pt (1.25 l) vacuum flask, pour in the mixed juice and syrup and top up with tonic or soda water. Swivel the flask before serving to mix the ingredients.

MEALS FOR TRAVELLERS

In days gone by it was possible to order packed luncheon baskets from the forefathers of British Rail Travellers-Fare. Such a picnic, truly a movable feast, might be enjoyed on even the shortest train journey and consisted according to one eye-witness of 'a cold collation, packed with chicken and a bottle of red or white wine, for a mere cost of 3s 6d'. As time passed, the pre-packed luncheon basket was replaced by restaurant carriages. Ironically, this kind of progress has now turned full circle. As the price of food rockets, more and more people will choose to bring their own travelling picnic.

Fortnum and Mason, of course, are old hands at providing food for travellers. This old family firm was supplying such delicacies as 'boned portions of poultry and game; eggs in brandy-soaked cake with whipped cream, and savoury patties', as long ago as 1788. Their supplies were manna from heaven to the forces (officers and gentlemen mostly) fighting in the Crimea, and equally acceptable to the members of the London gentlemen's clubs. It was for the latter that the concentrated luncheon or savoury lozenge was invented—almost certainly the first 'take-away'—'forming a desirable and portable Refreshment in travelling, hunting, shooting and other sports; they are also recommended to Members of Parliament, Gentlemen detained on Juries, or when long abstinence from meals is indispensable.'

Today Fortnum's is still the biggest name in take-away picnics, a familiar label on the hundreds of individually packed cardboard boxes that descend on such events as the Derby, Ascot, Wimbledon and the Test matches, and accompany travellers on their journeys to country estates. For very special occasions wicker picnic hampers, purchased from the store, are packed full of all the necessaries to keep body and soul alive: prime Scotch smoked salmon, sharply roasted spring chicken, champagne, and the inevitable strawberries and cream. The Head Chef at Fortnum's bears out what we have long ago suspected: that most wealthy people are unadventurous in their picnicking tastes, and prefer foie gras (£5 an ounce) and caviar (£150 a pound) to anything else.

Unlike Fortnum's, Harrods of Knightsbridge does not employ a team of chefs but rather an attractive young lady buyer who will whizz round the famous Food Hall and Wine Shop, selecting on your behalf all the choicest items and packing them neatly in a cardboard carry-

Cold meat and salad, roll and butter, and wine or beer were the mainstay of railway luncheon baskets from the 1870s, until restaurant cars came into widespread use *(Travellers-Fare)*

Fortnum & Mason picnic hamper *(Fortnum & Mason)*

Winston Churchill with Maj Gen John Anderson and Lt Gen Simpson at an impromptu lunch in Germany on 25 March 1945 *(Imperial War Museum)*

box with all the accompanying napkins, disposable cutlery and plates. In the summer they do a nice line in speciality picnics—the Howzat (for cricket), Brand's Hatch, Badminton, and Ascot luncheon. There is even a child's picnic, complete in mini Harrods PVC bag, containing yoghurt, crisps, fruit, napkins and a colouring book and crayons.

Many a small delicatessen will pack a picnic for you to make the journey pass more comfortably. So will hotels, though not all will go to the same trouble as The Lygon Arms in Broadway, which sends its guests out to sight-see armed with honey-roast ham, roast beef and chicken, and 'a chilled bottle of wine with the cork half drawn'. But if no such options are open to you, the next best idea is to pack your own 'movable feast'.

At this juncture, a word or two about sandwiches. A great deal has been written scorning the invention of John Montagu, fourth Earl of Sandwich. For it was he who first asked for his meat between two slices of bread so that he could linger longer at the gaming tables. Whatever you may think of his invention—and the way it has been subsequently expanded by the Americans on the one hand and compressed by institutional caterers on the other—it still remains a very useful way of binding all the necessary ingredients for a meal into one easily consumable handful.

A traveller's picnic can be very basic—indeed there are those who, like William Cobbett, eighteenth-century traveller extraordinary and author of *Rural Rides*, would agree that a diet of nuts and apples is 'excellent and most wholesome fare . . . upon average I have eaten a pint a day since I left home'.

Potted Prawns *(serves 4–6)*

5 oz (150 g) butter
8 oz (225 g) fresh cooked prawns, shelled
Large pinch of cayenne pepper
½ level teaspoon ground mace
Pinch of nutmeg
Freshly ground black pepper

Melt 4 oz (125 g) of the butter in a medium-sized saucepan. Add the prawns and the seasonings and heat together, stirring well so that the fish is impregnated with the butter.

Spoon into small ramekins or pots. Heat the remaining butter, clarify it by skimming or passing through a fine sieve, and pour over the top of the pots. Place in the refrigerator to chill until set, then pack into a lidded plastic container.

Avocado and Lemon Soup *(serves 6)*

4 lemons
3 ripe avocados
Small bunch of fresh parsley, chopped
1½ pt (850 ml) chicken stock
½ pt (250 ml) single cream
Salt and white pepper
Parsley to garnish

Squeeze the juice from 3 of the lemons. Peel the avocados, remove their stones and dip the fruit into the lemon juice as soon as it is exposed to the air. Put the avocado, lemon juice and parsley into a blender and mix thoroughly. Add the chicken stock (or as much as you can get into your blender goblet) and blend again. Mix in any remaining stock, the single cream and salt and pepper to taste.

Pour into a bowl, cover and chill for a few hours. With a sharp knife, score the remaining lemon lengthwise with a sharp knife to give a castellated effect, and cut into delicate slices. Put a lemon slice and a sprinkling of parsley into each cup or bowl before setting out; transfer the soup into a pre-chilled vacuum flask, and stack the bowls in the picnic basket with some clingfilm over the top. All you will have to do at the picnic site is pour the soup out.

71

Smoked Salmon and Crab Cornets *(serves 6)*

5 oz (150 g) crab meat (tinned
    frozen or, preferably, fresh)
2 tablespoons lemon juice
Cayenne pepper
5 fl oz (125 ml) single cream
2 eggs, separated

3 tablespoons sherry
½ oz (15 g) or 1 envelope gelatine
8 oz (225 g) smoked salmon
    (or 2 thin slivers per person)
Lettuce, parsley and lemon to
    garnish

Put crab meat in a bowl and pick over carefully to extract any shell or sinew. Add lemon juice and a dash of cayenne pepper and mix thoroughly.

Warm the cream carefully (using a double saucepan or asbestos mat if possible). Add egg yolks one by one, stirring all the time until mixture thickens. (If you over-heat it will curdle but a quick whizz in the blender should rectify this.)

Put the sherry in a teacup, add the gelatine and dissolve over hot water. Add to the cream and egg. Cool slightly and add to the crab meat. Beat the egg whites until stiff and fold into the crab mixture. Chill.

Spoon a dollop of the crab mousse onto each slice of smoked salmon and roll into a cornet shape. Lay the cornets in star formation on a bed of lettuce. Decorate with parsley and lemon slices, and cover with clingfilm.

Pâté en Croûte *(serves 4–6)*

2 oz (50 g) mushrooms, finely
    chopped
1 oz (25 g) butter
1 teaspoon brandy
8 oz (225 g) puff pastry

5 oz (125 g) pâté de foie
Beaten egg to glaze
¼ pt (150 ml) aspic flavoured
    with ½ level tablespoon apple
    juice or jelly

Cook the mushrooms gently in the butter to soften. Add the brandy and cool.

Roll out the pastry thinly to an oblong shape approximately 12 x 8 in (30 x 20 cm). Roll the pâté to an oblong shape approximately 8 x 5 in (20 x 13 cm). Spoon softened mushrooms down centre of pâté slab; draw edges of pâté up to form a roll.

Place pâté roll on pastry and fold up fairly loosely in parcel fashion, sealing edges with water. Turn upside-down onto a greased baking sheet so that the join in the pastry is underneath. Make a hole in the centre of the parcel and insert a small roll of greaseproof paper to keep the hole open during the baking.

Decorate with pastry trimmings and brush with beaten egg. Bake in the centre of a hot oven (400°F, 200°C; Gas Mark 6) for about 30 minutes until golden brown.

Make up the aspic flavoured with apple juice or jelly. When pastry is cooked, remove paper roll and pour in aspic through a funnel. (If any aspic is left over pour it onto a plate and leave to set in refrigerator. When set, chop with a knife to use as decoration.)

Chill pâté roll in refrigerator until needed. Wrap carefully in foil, already sliced for ease of serving.

Individual Smoked Haddock Flans *(makes 6)*

6 oz (175 g) plain flour
Large pinch of salt
Pinch of cayenne pepper
3 oz (75 g) butter
3 oz (75 g) Cheddar cheese, grated
1 egg yolk
2 eggs
1/4 pt (150 ml) single cream

Grated rind and juice of
  1/2 lemon
Pinch of mustard powder
7 oz (200 g) smoked haddock, cooked, skinned and flaked
1 tablespoon fresh parsley, chopped
Lemon slices to garnish

Sift together the flour, salt and cayenne pepper. Rub in the butter until the mixture resembles fine breadcrumbs. Add the grated cheese and mix thoroughly. Beat the egg yolk lightly and mix into the pastry to form a stiff dough. Knead lightly on a floured surface and leave it to rest, covered, in the refrigerator for 30 minutes.

Roll out the pastry thinly and line 6 flan tins each 4 in (10 cm) in diameter. Line with foil or greaseproof paper and bake 'blind' in a hot oven (400°F, 200°C; Gas Mark 6) for 15 minutes, uncovering the pastry for the last 5 minutes.

Beat together the eggs, cream, lemon rind and juice, and the mustard powder. Add the flaked haddock and parsley and spoon carefully into the flan cases. Bake in a moderate oven (350°F; 180°C; Gas Mark 4) for 20–25 minutes until set. Cool and garnish with lemon twists.

Pack into a greaseproof-lined sandwich box. If stacked in layers, protect with strips of greaseproof paper.

Savoury Scotch Eggs *(makes 4 eggs)*

5 eggs
4 level tablespoons dry sage and onion stuffing
1/4 pt (150 ml) boiling water
12 oz (350 g) sausagemeat

A little flour
2 oz (50 g) fresh white breadcrumbs
Cooking oil for deep frying

Hard boil 4 of the eggs for 10 minutes then plunge immediately into cold water. Make up the stuffing with the boiling water; add to the sausagemeat and mix well.

Shell the eggs and dust each one with flour. Divide the sausagemeat into four chunks and mould ¼ round each egg, smoothing over all the joins.

Beat the remaining egg and dip in each Scotch egg before covering in breadcrumbs. Make sure each egg is thickly and evenly coated. Fry in deep fat for 10–15 minutes or until the eggs are golden brown all over. Drain, cool and chill before packing into the picnic box.

Veal, Bacon and Parsley Pie *(serves 6)*

1 lb (450 g) bacon joint, pre-soaked	½ teaspoon salt
12 oz (350 g) stewing veal, trimmed	Freshly ground black pepper
	1 lb (450 g) plain flour
2 tablespoons fresh parsley, chopped	1 teaspoon salt
	5 oz (150 g) lard
1 small onion, finely chopped	⅓ pt (175 ml) water
Grated rind and juice of ½ lemon	Beaten egg to glaze
	½ pt (250 ml) aspic jelly

Cut the bacon and veal into small cubes and mix with the parsley, onion, rind and juice of lemon, salt and pepper.

To make the hot-water crust pastry, first sift the flour and salt together in a bowl, then heat the lard and water in a saucepan until the fat melts. Bring to the boil and pour at once into the flour. Stir to form a soft paste. Turn onto a lightly-floured board and knead until smooth.

While the pastry is still warm, cut off ⅓ and keep warm and well covered. Roll out the remaining pastry to a 12 in (30 cm) diameter circle and use to line a 6 in (15 cm) loose-bottomed cake tin.

Press the filling into the pastry case and roll the remaining pastry to make a lid. Moisten the pastry edges well before putting the lid in place. Make a hole in the centre and use any surplus pastry to decorate the top. Brush with beaten egg and bake in a hot oven (450°F, 230°C; Gas Mark 8) for 15 minutes, reducing the heat to very moderate (325°F, 160°C; Gas Mark 3) for a further 2 hours until the meat is tender.

Leave to cool in the tin, but while still warm pour in some of the melted aspic jelly through a funnel. Cut the pie into slices, wrap carefully in foil and keep chilled if possible.

Cold Stuffed Courgettes *(serves 4)*

4 medium-sized courgettes	A dash of Worcestershire sauce
2 oz (50 g) ham, minced	2 spring onions, finely chopped
1 oz (25 g) cheese, grated	1 small tomato, skinned and chopped
Salt and freshly ground black pepper	Large pinch of thyme

Wash and dry the courgettes and using an apple corer, remove as much of the middle of each courgette as you can, digging in from either end.

Mix the remaining ingredients together and spoon into the cavities. Wrap each courgette in lightly-greased foil, place in a small roasting tin or casserole and bake in a medium oven (350°F, 180°C; Gas Mark 4) for about 1 hour. When cool, transfer to the refrigerator and chill.

Spiced Chicken Salad *(serves 6)*

1 cup long grain rice
2 cups water
1/2 level teaspoon salt
12 oz (350 g) cooked chicken, diced
1 red eating apple, cored, chopped and dipped in lemon
2 oz (50 g) currants
4 oz (125 g) button mushrooms, sliced
1/2 bunch of spring onions, chopped
1/2 green pepper, seeded and chopped
1/2 tablespoon caster sugar
1 teaspoon French mustard
6 tablespoons salad oil
2 tablespoons lemon juice
Salt and freshly ground black pepper
1/2 oz (15 g) butter
1 oz (25 g) flaked almonds

Put the rice in a pan with the water and salt and bring to the boil. Cover and simmer for about 10 minutes or until the rice is just tender. Drain and dry out in the oven if necessary.

Combine the chicken, apple, currants, mushrooms and spring onions in a mixing bowl. Blanch the pepper, drain well and add to the mixture. Fold in the rice while still warm.

Put the sugar, mustard, oil and lemon juice in a screw-top jar, season with salt and freshly ground pepper and blend thoroughly by giving the jar a vigorous shaking. Stir into the warm rice salad and mix so that all the grains of rice are coated with the dressing. Melt the butter and fry the almonds until golden brown. Spoon portions of the salad into individual dishes, scatter the almonds on top and chill until required.

Sandwiches

Sandwiches are the ultimate in fast food. With all the ingredients to hand you can make a sandwich in under a minute and that beats a hamburger anyday. They are even quite good for you—some dieticians say that fresh sandwiches with adequate savoury fillings can be just as satisfying as a sit-down dinner. When they fail to please it tends to be because of poor quality bread and, at least on this side of the Atlantic, a less-than-generous filling.

Open sandwiches are discussed more fully in the next chapter; but the same requirement applies whether they have a lid or not. First, it is absolutely essential to use good bread with some 'guts' in it. Limp and soggy sliced bread has no taste, no texture and does not hold its shape for long if used with a substantial filling. Gutsy breads such as Farmhouse, Bloomer, Wholemeal, Wheatgerm and Granary are the ones to use.

Secondly, the bread should be thinly sliced; and this is easier to achieve when it is not fresh from the baker's oven. Find a good baker with a slicing machine and all your sandwich problems are over. Thirdly, remember to butter the bread all over, right up to the crusts. The butter acts as a protective layer to stop the filling juices from making the bread soggy.

Choose your sandwich fillings according to the type of picnic, certainly, but also according to how long they will remain uneaten.

Freezer Sandwiches
According to the experts, sandwiches should be stored in a home freezer for a maximum of 2 months. They should be sealed in polythene bags, boxes or foil, and labelled with the quantity, type of filling and date frozen. To thaw, leave at room temperature for 2–3 hours, or overnight in a refrigerator. Avoid fillings that have any kind of salad ingredient, are spicy or well-seasoned, flavoured with mayonnaise or containing hard-boiled egg. It is best to keep frozen sandwiches fairly plain, using cheese, meat or fish combined with cream cheese or softened butter to make a tasty, moist spread. Try the following fillings.

Cream cheese, nuts and raisins
Mix 4 oz (125 g) cream cheese with 1 oz (25 g) chopped walnuts or salted peanuts and 1 oz (25 g) raisins.

Prawn and cream cheese
Mix 4 oz (125 g) roughly chopped prawns with 2 oz (50 g) cream cheese, 1 teaspoon lemon juice, salt and just a touch of cayenne pepper.

Chicken and ham
Bind together 4 oz (125 g) chopped cooked chicken and 2 oz (50 g) chopped ham with 2 oz (50 g) softened butter, and season with salt and freshly ground black pepper. Sprinkle with chopped fresh parsley.

Smoked salmon and anchovy
Mix 4 oz (125 g) smoked salmon pieces with 2 oz (50 g) butter and a smear of anchovy paste.

Made-the-night-before Sandwiches

Most sandwiches are edible if made the night before the picnic; but some are more edible than others. As a general rule avoid cucumber, sliced tomatoes, fruit, wet ham or bloody beef. You can just get away with lettuce if the leaves have been thoroughly dried beforehand.

Coronation chicken
Mix 4 oz (125 g) cooked, finely chopped chicken with 2 tablespoons mayonnaise, 1 teaspoon sweet chutney and ¼ teaspoon curry paste.

Devilled ham
Mix 4 oz (125 g) cooked, minced ham with 1 teaspoon Worcestershire sauce, ¼ teaspoon made mustard, salt and freshly ground black pepper, and bind together with 1 oz (25 g) softened butter.

Pork, apple and celery
Chop 3 or 4 slices of pork into bite-sized pieces and bind with 2 teaspoons apple jelly, 1 tablespoon chopped celery, plus salt, pepper and a pinch of thyme.

Salmon, egg and watercress
Make watercress butter by blending 2 oz (50 g) butter with a few chopped sprigs of watercress. Scramble 1 egg, mix in 1 tablespoon mayonnaise and 3 oz (75 g) skinned, boned and flaked salmon (canned). Spread one slice with the butter, the other with the salmon and eggs, and join together.

Morning-only Sandwiches

Real sandwich afficionados maintain that the only way to enjoy the food at its best is to make it and eat it immediately. Should you claim acquaintance with such dedicated individuals and feel inclined to invite them on your picnic, you are undoubtedly advised to pack up bread and fillings separately and let the company make their own sandwiches. Failing that, make them on the morning of departure. The following fillings at any rate should never be made up before:

Cottage cheese, ham and peach
Mix 3 oz (75 g) cottage cheese with 2 oz (50 g) minced ham and ¼ fresh peach, chopped. Bind the mixture with 1 tablespoon of mayonnaise and season with salt and pepper.

Tuna, mint and cucumber
Remove the skin from ¼ cucumber, chop it, sprinkle with salt and leave to drain for 1 hour at least. Drain a 7 oz (200 g) can of tuna fish, flake and mix with 2 tablespoons mayonnaise and 2 teaspoons mint

sauce. Add the drained cucumber, season to taste and spread on well-buttered bread.

Banana, honey and walnut
Thinly slice 1 banana, dip in lemon juice and mix with 1 tablespoon thick honey, 1 oz (25 g) chopped walnuts and a few sultanas.

Chilli beef
Combine 4 oz (125 g) minced roast beef with 3 tablespoons tomato ketchup, 1 teaspoon marmite or Bovril and a large pinch of chilli powder.

General points
Wrap different flavoured sandwiches separately so that the flavours do not mix.
Soften or cream the butter to make it go further, and flavour with curry paste, tomato purée, mustard, horseradish or parsley, for added interest.

Chocolate and Orange Mousse *(serves 4)*

3 oz (75 g) plain chocolate	2 teaspoons powdered gelatine
3 eggs, separated	¼ pt (150 ml) double cream
Grated rind and juice of 1 orange	Whipped cream and chocolate
3 oz (75 g) caster sugar	curls to decorate

Melt the chocolate in a heatproof basin over a saucepan of hot water. Beat the egg yolks, orange rind and sugar to a thick cream. Dissolve the gelatine in the orange juice by heating in a cup standing in hot water. Allow to cool slightly and stir into the sugar cream along with the melted chocolate.

Whip the double cream until just stiff and fold into the chocolate mixture. Whip the egg whites until stiff and fold in these also. Spoon into 4 portions in 3 fl oz (90 ml) ramekins or individual foil dishes and leave to set in the refrigerator. If liked, decorate with whipped cream and chocolate curls, and cover with clingfilm.

Sour Cream and Raisin Flan *(serves 4–6)*

2 oz (50 g) butter or margarine	½ oz (15 g) caster sugar
1 oz (25 g) soft brown sugar	¼ pt (150 ml) sour cream
6 oz (175 g) muesli	2 teaspoons lemon juice
3 tablespoons water	2 oz (50 g) seedless raisins
2 large eggs	

Heat the butter in a medium-sized saucepan. Mix in the sugar and cook gently until it has dissolved. Add the muesli, stir in thoroughly;

add the water and mix again. Spoon the mixture into a greased 7 in (18 cm) flan tin (preferably foil for ease of carrying) and press it into the base and sides of the tin to make a firm flan case. Put in the refrigerator to chill for 10 minutes.

Beat the eggs with the caster sugar until thick and frothy. Stir in the sour cream and lemon juice. Sprinkle the raisins over the base of the chilled flan case; pour over the egg mixture and bake in a very moderate oven (325°F, 160°C; Gas Mark 3) for 20–25 minutes until the filling is just set.

Allow to cool and chill until required. The flan can be cut in wedges before the picnic and transported in a rigid plastic container, or taken to the site in the flan tin.

Fruited Bran Loaf

2 oz (50 g) bran
5 oz (150 g) brown sugar
8 oz (225 g) dried fruit

½ pt (250 ml) milk
6 oz (175 g) self-raising flour

Put the bran, sugar and dried fruit into a bowl and mix thoroughly. Stir in the milk, sift in the flour and mix well. Pour into a well-greased 1 lb (450 g) loaf tin and bake in a moderate oven (350°F, 180°C; Gas Mark 4) for 1 ¼ hours.

When the loaf is cooked, turn it out of the tin and cool on a wire rack. Cut into thick slices, spread with farmhouse butter and wrap in foil, sandwiching the slices together to conserve the butter. Not only does this fruit loaf taste delicious, it is good for you as well.

Hot Coffee Punch *(serves 6)*

8 tablespoons coarsely ground
    coffee
Pared rind and juice of 1 orange
1 teaspoon cinnamon
3 tablespoons brown sugar

1 ¾ pt (1 l) water
4 fl oz (100 ml) brandy
¼ pt (150 ml) whipped cream
Grated chocolate to decorate

Measure the coffee into a large coffee jug. Add the pared orange rind, cinnamon, and sugar. Boil the water and pour it into the jug, stir and stand in a warm place for 5–8 minutes. Strain into a pre-heated thermos flask together with the orange juice, then add the brandy.

Carry the whipped cream separately in a lidded plastic pot, and the grated chocolate in a twist of clingfilm. To serve, pour out a cup of coffee punch and top with whipped cream and grated chocolate.

FÊTES CHAMPÊTRES

Fête champêtre means 'a rural festival or entertainment'. In such a clime as ours, the marshalling of large numbers of people, at a given place and a given hour, is invariably fraught with problems. Nonetheless the National Trust has, in the past few years, organised some of the most spectacular *fêtes champêtres*. Thanks to them we can enjoy the occasion more or less as it was originally intended.

Not surprisingly the idea began across the Channel, where the creation of the great gardens of Europe in the seventeenth and eighteenth centuries led to a passion for outdoor entertaining in the grand manner. In France, Le Nôtre laid out the elaborate gardens of Versailles for Louis XIV, and it was here that the style was set for the grandest *fête champêtre* of all.

In the palace grounds, ballrooms, supper rooms and boudoirs were artificially created, using lavish hedges and trees to form their walls, with painted canvas pavilions to keep out the rain. The principle was similar to the British preoccupation of the time with temples and gazebos; in other words, translating the indoors to the outdoors by creating outside eating and living areas. In Versailles today you can still see the layout of the garden ballroom.

The principal feature of a *fête champêtre* was the picnic, the idea being that guests brought their own food and 'discovered' delightful spots to eat it in. Entertainments, surprises, and jokes of all kinds were devised to keep the merrymakers happy. Fancy dress was often worn in keeping with a given theme.

Unfortunately for some, the joke element could often be quite nasty. All sorts of tricks were played on the guests, from a mild soaking brought about by concealed jets of water, released by a footstep on a paving stone; to a really terrifying encounter with a pit-full of be-jewelled 'snakes' hissing jets of steam, into which the hapless guests were precipitated.

The British adopted the *fête champêtre* with great enthusiasm—though perhaps with less hedonism—and developed the idea into the pleasure park entertainments of eighteenth-century London. In Vauxhall Gardens, fashionable society came to enjoy lavish illumination of lamps and flambeaux, the music of Mozart and Haydn, the topical glees and ballads, the fireworks, fountains, nightingales, wine and food, picnics and masked company. Horace Walpole described a

The interior of the Temple of the Winds at Mount Stewart, Co Down. During the eighteenth century such buildings were used for lavish outdoor entertaining *(Patrick Rossmore)* and *inset* the exterior *(The National Trust)*

'splendid jubilee-masquerade' in 1749, with 'various bands of music disposed in different parts and a great display of fireworks.' He arrived by barge with a fanfare of French horns!

In the great country houses, parks were elaborately designed to give excitement and pleasure to their owners and countless fashionable guests. Picnics were carefully devised without elaborate trappings, though hosts were not above planting grassy banks with carpets of daisies and pansies to create an overnight 'natural' effect.

Stourhead, the National Trust property in Wiltshire, has survived as a perfect example of an eighteenth-century garden. Designed with great imagination by Henry Hoare the banker, it was inspired by his grand tours of Italy and the romantic landscapes of Claude Lorrain and Gaspard Poussin. The concept was linked with the journey of Aeneas into the underworld, and the literary associations of Virgil's *Aeneid*. From all this a magnificent landscape was formed complete with temples, a Pantheon and a Grotto dedicated to the Nymphs of the Grot. The follies were linked by winding paths in the most natural style; a rockwork bridge was cunningly constructed so that visitors thought they were climbing a stony bank; while another route led through a mysterious subterranean tunnel.

This setting lent itself splendidly to family outdoor parties and to *fêtes champêtres*, which the National Trust has now recreated at Stourhead, as well as at Petworth in West Sussex, Claremont in Surrey and some of its other landscape gardens. The programmes are based on eighteenth-century entertainments, on singers, dancers, jugglers and sideshows. Thousands of people come along, just as they would have done to an eighteenth-century pleasure garden. There are musical interludes, fireworks and, of course, picnics of every shape, size and description.

Another event which seems to attract the grand style of outdoor eating is Glyndebourne. Ever since this unique opera house was founded in 1934, it has encouraged its patrons to either picnic in the beautiful gardens or dine in the restaurant during the long interval of each performance.

It is very much an occasion for those who like to see and be seen. The form is to arrive attired in evening dress suitably early for a performance that starts around 5.00 pm. If you choose to picnic, you rush immediately into the gardens to 'bag' the best spots and cool your wine in the lake.

When preparing a *fête champêtre*, keep your offering light and fanciful rather than heavy and leaden—especially if a gentle amble round the grounds is to follow, or the second half of a play or opera. There is nothing like too much food and wine to induce lethargy; or worse still, snores of Rip Van Winkle proportions that have an uncanny ability of being heard over even the loudest chorus.

Cold Vichyssoise Soup *(serves 12–14)*

2 lb (900 g) leeks, washed,
  trimmed and sliced
12 oz (350 g) potatoes, peeled
  and diced
1½ pt (750 ml) chicken stock
1 teaspoon dried tarragon

Salt and pepper
½ pt (250 ml) milk
½ pt (250 ml) double cream
Bunch of chives, finely chopped
½ pt (250 ml) natural yoghurt
  or sour cream

Prepare the vegetables. Bring the stock to the boil and add leeks, potatoes, tarragon and seasonings to the pan. Return to the boil, cover and simmer gently for about 10–15 minutes or until the vegetables are tender.

Purée the contents of the pan in a blender, together with the milk, double cream and half the chopped chives. (Unless you have an enormous blender or food processor you will have to do this in three stages, blending a third of the mixture in one go.)

Cover and chill for several hours. Keep cold in an ice box until needed. Serve, if possible, in a large glass or silver bowl. Swirl in the yoghurt or sour cream at the last minute to give a marbled appearance and sprinkle remaining chopped chives on top.

Orange and Pineapple Salad Starter *(serves 10–12)*

1 large or 2 small pineapples
2 juicy oranges
1 lemon
Large pinch of salt

1 cos lettuce
Caster sugar
Mint to decorate

Cut the pineapple into chunks, discarding skin and central hard core. Peel the oranges, remove the pith and pips, and divide into segments, cutting each segment in half.

Grate the rind from the lemon; squeeze the juice and mix together with the rind and salt. Pour over the fruit, mix well, and leave to stand overnight.

Line a pretty, portable serving bowl with the lettuce leaves. Pile the orange and pineapple salad into the bowl, sprinkle with caster sugar and decorate with mint leaves. Cover with clingfilm and chill until needed.

This is good served as a salad with fatty meats such as pork or duck.

Sole in Curry Mayonnaise *(serves 10–12)*

10 large fillets of sole
¼ pt (150 ml) dry white wine
¼ pt (150 ml) water
Salt and white pepper

1 rounded teaspoon tomato
  purée
1 teaspoon caster sugar
Juice of ½ lemon

2 tablespoons olive oil
1 small onion, finely chopped
1 clove garlic, crushed
1 level tablespoon curry powder

¾ pt (400 ml) mayonnaise
3 tablespoons single cream
Parsley, slices of lemon and raw
   mushrooms to garnish

Cut each fillet into strips; poach in the wine and water, with a shake of salt and pepper, for about 8 minutes. Drain the fish but retain the stock.

Heat the oil in a large, heavy frying pan, and cook the onion and garlic gently until soft and transparent. Add the curry powder and cook for a minute or two longer. Then add the tomato purée, sugar, lemon juice and ¼ pt (150 ml) of the poaching liquid. Simmer gently until the mixture is thick and most of the liquid has evaporated.

Cool the sauce, then add the mayonnaise and cream. Arrange the poached fish in a light dish or casserole and pour over the sauce. Garnish, just before setting out, with sprigs of parsley, twists of lemon and slices of raw mushrooms. Keep covered and cool until required. Serve with a plain rice salad.

Chicken, Ham and Tongue Galantine *(serves 6–8)*

1 large fresh chicken (4–5 lb/
   1.8–2.3 kg)
1 small onion
8 oz (225 g) pie veal
8 oz (225 g) lean pork
Salt and freshly ground black
   pepper

Sherry-glassful of dry sherry
1 oz (25 g) walnuts, finely
   chopped
1 egg, beaten
4 oz (125 g) sliced ham
4 oz (125 g) sliced tongue
6 stuffed olives

Bone the chicken, or even better ask a friendly butcher to do it for you. Chop the onion finely and mince the veal and pork. Mix onion, minced meats, seasoning, sherry and walnuts in a bowl; bind with the beaten egg.

Cut the ham and tongue into strips. Place the boned chicken on a board and layer the stuffing, ham and tongue strips and olives inside it. Using fine string, sew up the apertures and mould it by hand into a smooth, oval shape.

Brush the surface of the chicken with some cooking oil, season with more salt and pepper, and roast in a moderately hot oven (400°F, 200°C; Gas Mark 6) for about 1½ hours. For the first hour, cover the chicken parcel with greaseproof paper or foil so that it does not dry out and become over-brown.

When cooked, allow to cool with a weight on top. If possible, leave overnight in the refrigerator until compacted. Serve sliced with plenty of green salad, crusty bread and tomato cups filled with thickened mayonnaise (see page 86).

Raised Pork Pie *(serves 6–8)*

For the jelly stock:
2 pigs trotters or 2 lb (900 g)
   veal bones chopped
1 carrot
1 small onion stuck with 4 cloves
1 clove garlic, crushed
Sprig of thyme
6 peppercorns
Cold water

For the pastry:
12 oz (350 g) plain flour
½ teaspoon salt
4 oz (125 g) lard
¼ pt (150 ml) milk and water
   mixed

For the filling:
1½ lb (675 g) pork shoulder or
   end pieces of unsmoked bacon
Onion salt
White pepper
½ teaspoon dried sage
¼ teaspoon dried parsley
1 tablespoon lemon juice
½ teaspoon anchovy essence

To glaze:
Beaten egg

Two days before the picnic make the jelly stock by putting the trotters or bones in a saucepan; add carrot, onion, garlic and seasonings, covering with cold water. With a lid on the pan bring to the boil, removing the scum as it appears. Simmer for 3–4 hours. (It is best to do this a couple of days beforehand so that if you have any doubts about the setting quality of the jelly—for example in very hot weather—you can add gelatine.)

To make the pastry, sift the flour and salt together. Melt the lard in a saucepan with the milk/water; make a well in the centre of the flour, pour in the liquid, and work until you have a smooth dough. Knead well, then cut off a third for the pie lid, cover and keep warm over boiling water.

Press the remainder round the base and sides of a wetted, straight-sided 2 lb (900 g) jar, or a small cake tin, until the pastry forms an even case with walls about ¼ in (6 mm) thick. Put aside to 'set' while you prepare the pork.

Trim pork of most of the fat and mince on a coarse blade. Season with salt, pepper and herbs; stir in the lemon juice and anchovy essence and mix thoroughly. Remove jar from the pastry case and pack meat in to within ¾ in (19 mm) of the top.

Roll out the remaining pastry and use as a lid for the case, remembering to damp the edges with cold water. Pinch the join together tightly and push up to form a ridge. Make a hole in the top and glaze with beaten egg.

Stand the pie on a greased baking sheet and fix a piece of buttered greaseproof paper round it, like a collar, to keep its shape during cooking. Bake in the centre of a moderately hot oven (400°F, 200°C; Gas

Mark 6) for 1 hour, reducing the temperature (325°F, 160°C; Gas Mark 3) for a further 1–1½ hours.

Leave to cool before pouring melted jelly stock into the pie through a funnel. Allow to set in the refrigerator. Pack the pie well to protect the pastry crust and keep the paper collar on until you are about to serve it.

Moulding your own pork pie takes practice if you are to achieve the perfect shape, but a degree of 'middle-age-spread' at least shows you made it yourself! Alternatively you could buy a tin mould to bake it in—far simpler but less traditional.

Aspic Jelly
In general terms, there are three ways of making aspic jelly. The first is the proper way, similar to the jellied stock in Raised Pork Pie (see page 85), which involves the lengthy boiling of bones in flavoured stock. In Victorian and Edwardian times, when aspic was the *sine qua non* of any picnic food, this was an enormously extravagant performance. Charles Francatelli's recipe (he who was chef at one time to Queen Victoria) states: 'Take 30 pounds of fresh veal and put it into a stock pot together with 4 hens and 18 calves' feet previously boned and par-boiled for 10 minutes. Fill up the stock pot with 4 gallons of water . . .'.

No wonder that Kettner wrote in his *Book of the Table*, published in 1877, that 'In England especially, where cold meats are in great request, the monotony of aspic is too palpable.'

Nevertheless, it has to be admitted that aspic can be quite a useful ingredient. It lends itself to all sorts of different flavours; is essential in chicken or turkey pies, where the meat has little natural jelly; and is useful for thickening mayonnaise or setting firm savoury jellies which the rigours of travelling can reduce to a floppy mess.

The second method is from a packet and, setting aside your finer feelings, is very useful when time is short. The third way, which has much to recommend it, is a combination of 'instant' and effort:

For 1 pt (500 ml) aspic jelly

½ oz (15 g) leaf gelatine (available in high class grocers/ delicatessens, and generally thought superior to powder)	¾ pt (400 ml) beef stock, hot 2 tablespoons dry sherry A squeeze of lemon juice

Soak the gelatine in a little water. Add remaining ingredients and stir until dissolved. Chill and use as required.

Collared Beef in Red Wine Jelly *(serves 10–12)*

5–6 lb (2.3–2.7 kg) silverside or boned and rolled fore-rib of beef
Salt and freshly ground black pepper
1/2 teaspoon mixed spice
1/4 teaspoon dried thyme
1/4 teaspoon powdered sage
2 bayleaves
1 teaspoon cloves
1 medium onion, chopped
1 clove garlic, crushed
1 pt (500 ml) red wine
1 envelope gelatine
Fresh parsley and radish roses to garnish

Wipe and trim the beef and sprinkle with salt and pepper. Mix the spice, thyme and sage, and rub into the meat. Place beef, bayleaves, cloves, onion and garlic in a large saucepan. Pour over the wine and marinate for at least 12 hours, turning occasionally.

Heat the contents of the saucepan until boiling, then cover and simmer for about 3 hours. Allow to cool, then drain the beef. Cover with a small plate and press down with a heavy weight. Set aside to chill in the refrigerator.

Strain and skim the red wine stock. Return it to the pan and bring to the boil for a few minutes. Dissolve the gelatine in it, season to taste and allow to cool until setting point is reached.

Slice the chilled beef, arrange the slices on a large platter and spoon the syrupy jelly over each slice. Garnish with sprigs of fresh parsley and radish roses. Cover with clingfilm until required.

Honey-crusted Lamb *(serves 8–10)*

6 tablespoons oil
3 tablespoons lemon juice
2 or 3 sprigs of fresh rosemary
1 clove garlic, crushed
1 teaspoon salt
Freshly ground black pepper
1 lean, tender leg of lamb
2–3 tablespoons thin honey
2 oz (50 g) fresh white breadcrumbs
1 small onion, finely chopped
Watercress to decorate

Prepare a marinade by mixing oil, lemon juice, all but 1 teaspoon of chopped rosemary, crushed garlic, 1/2 teaspoon salt and some black pepper. Pour over the lamb and leave for 4–5 hours.

Drain and pat the lamb dry with kitchen paper. Spread with honey. Mix breadcrumbs with the onion, remaining rosemary (finely chopped) and some more salt and black pepper. Spread over the lamb and roast in a moderate oven (375°F, 190°C; Gas Mark 5) for 30 minutes per lb (450 g) or until the meat is cooked as desired.

Cool quickly and chill in the refrigerator. The meat could be served pre-sliced and set out on a platter decorated with watercress.

Cold lamb can be fatty and quite nasty if not carefully chosen, so above all go for quality rather than quantity.

Saffron, Orange and Nut Rice Salad *(serves 10–12)*

4 cups long grain rice
8 cups water
2 teaspoons salt
1 packet saffron strands
1 orange
¼ pt (150 ml) salad oil
2 tablespoons white wine
   vinegar

Salt and freshly ground black
   pepper
4 oz (125 g) raisins
Small bunch of spring onions,
   chopped
2 oz (50 g) flaked almonds,
   roughly chopped
Chopped fresh parsley to garnish

Cook the rice in the water with the salt and saffron until barely tender (about 10 minutes but check after 8, because some types of rice cook more quickly than others).

Grate the rind of the orange finely, and squeeze the juice. While the rice is cooking, make dressing by putting oil, vinegar, orange juice, grated rind, salt, pepper into a screw-top jar and shaking vigorously.

While the rice is still hot, combine with the raisins and chopped spring onions. Pour over the dressing and toss thoroughly. Pile into a large serving bowl, sprinkle with flaked almonds and chopped parsley. Keep chilled and covered until required.

Moulded Tomato and Cucumber Salad *(serves up to 10)*

3 lb (1.4 kg) tomatoes
1 clove garlic, crushed
1 small onion, chopped
1 level tablespoon caster sugar
1 tablespoon tomato purée
Juice of ½ lemon
½ level teaspoon dried tarragon

1 teaspoon salt
Freshly ground black pepper
½ pt (250 ml) light stock
1½ envelopes gelatine
¼ cucumber
Watercress to garnish

Chop the tomatoes roughly and place in a large saucepan along with the garlic, onion, sugar, tomato purée, lemon juice, tarragon, salt and pepper. Add half the stock and cook gently for about 1 hour.

Dissolve the gelatine in remaining stock. Sieve the tomato mixture to remove all the skins and seeds. Add the dissolved gelatine and allow to cool.

Spoon a ½ in (1 cm) layer of tomato jelly into the base of a 2½ pt (1.5 l) ring mould. Place in a tray of ice and put into the refrigerator to set quickly. Prevent the remaining jelly from setting, meanwhile, by keeping warm over hot water.

Scallop the edges of the cucumber and slice thinly. Arrange the slices decoratively on the jelly layer. Spoon over another thin layer of liquid jelly and return to the refrigerator until set.

Finally, add remaining liquid jelly and leave in the refrigerator for

3–4 hours until set firm. To unmould, quickly dip the ring in hot water and invert onto a serving plate or container. Fill the centre with watercress.

Mayonnaise
Once the bane of the inexperienced cook's existence, mayonnaise is now, thanks to blenders with drip caps, as easy to make as a cup of tea. There is an additional advantage in using a blender, too—whereas the more traditional recipe demands the use of 2 egg yolks, in a blender you need only use 1 whole egg because the rapid whisking of the beaters ensures a smoother emulsion.

Straight mayonnaise (makes 1/2 pt [250 ml])
Break 1 egg into the blender goblet, add 2 tablespoons wine vinegar, salt and pepper, and 1/2 teaspoon French mustard. Blend at high speed for a few minutes, then gradually drip through 1/2 pt (250 ml) good oil (preferably olive).

If you haven't a drip cap on your blender, you can approximate by covering the blender goblet with foil and making a few tiny holes for the oil to drip through. The important thing is to keep the blender whisking at high speed and to ensure that the oil is added in a slow, steady stream.

Family mayonnaise (makes 1 pt [500 ml])
Children, particularly, do not enjoy foods that are too oily, and so find this version more to their taste.

Prepare as above, but when fully blended empty an 8 oz (225 g) tub of cottage cheese into the goblet and continue whisking until the mixture is smooth. Thin, if necessary, with single cream, yoghurt or top of the milk.

Garlic mayonnaise
Garlic is but one of the many flavourings that can be blended into mayonnaise (see Prawns in Aïoli page 43). Herbs such as parsley, tarragon, marjoram and chervil also 'lift' mayonnaise; as do chopped gherkins, olives or capers.

To rescue mayonnaise
Just in case the worst happens: break a fresh egg yolk into a clean blender goblet and beat in the curdled mixture a little at a time.

Open Sandwiches
A good open sandwich depends on four basic ingredients for its success. These are: a) the bread, which should be firm rather than floppy; b) the cream base or spread that will glue the topping to the

base; c) the topping which should be the main ingredient and strive to catch the eye; d) the garnish or flourish of colour on top. The following team up rather well:

Bread	Base	Topping	Garnish
Light rye	butter with a squeeze of lemon juice	thinly sliced smoked salmon	sprig of fresh dill and piped mayonnaise
	butter and whipped cream with a dash of horseradish	smoked eel or trout	cucumber and chopped pimento
	cream cheese	prawns and shredded lettuce	twisted lemon slice
	butter and sour cream	sliced roast beef	asparagus spears
	butter, then chopped ham and mayonnaise	sliced raw mushrooms	green pepper strips and a tomato quarter
	butter, then mashed liver sausage and mayonnaise	chopped crisp bacon	tomato slices
	butter	lettuce, cottage cheese mixed with chopped nuts	apple slices dipped in lemon juice
Dark rye	butter	pickled herring and sliced hard-boiled egg	orange twist, watercress sprig
	butter, then chopped chicken and mayonnaise	shelled prawns	lemon twists, parsley
	butter and potato salad	slices of tongue	sliced tomatoes
	cream cheese	sliced pineapple	watercress sprigs and crushed walnuts
	butter and horseradish	slice of ham rolled around chopped prunes	orange twist

Bread	Base	Topping	Garnish
Dark rye	butter	sliced liver sausage	pickled gherkins and crisp bacon
	butter and sour cream	thin slices of pork	shredded red cabbage, chopped apple dipped in lemon juice and chopped nuts
French bread (sliced across, at an angle, about ½ in (1 cm) thick, lightly toasted and cooled)	butter then chopped hard-boiled egg and mayonnaise	salami slices	tomato quarters and chopped chives
	butter and mayonnaise	crab, shredded lettuce, chopped gherkins	sliced raw mushrooms
	butter and chopped ham	lettuce, slices of blue cheese	salted peanuts
	parsley butter	chicken slices	tomato and chopped capers
	butter and sour cream	roast beef slices	tomato and sliced olive
	butter, then liver paté	slices of boiled ham	chopped pine-apple sprinkled with mint
	cream cheese	sliced tomato and chopped spring onion	freshly ground black pepper and chopped fresh basil
Crispbread (spread base thickly to prevent juices from soaking through)	parsley butter	chopped lettuce, sardine	lumpfish roe, lemon twist and tomato
	butter and horseradish	chopped cooked white fish, mayonnaise and lettuce strips	sliced hard-boiled egg and red pepper
	butter and cream cheese	sliced radishes	chopped chives
	butter and curry-flavoured mayonnaise	tomato slices	asparagus tips and chopped capers

91

Bread	Base	Topping	Garnish
Crispbread (spread base thickly to prevent juices from soaking through)	lemon-flavoured butter	thinly sliced smoked salmon	hard-boiled egg and a spoonful of lumpfish roe
	butter and pickle	thin slices of corned beef	chopped cucumber and tomato with a sprig of parsley
	butter and mayonnaise	lettuce, Swiss cheese	peeled black grapes

Tipsy Strawberries in Meringue Nests *(makes 8–10 nests)*

4 egg whites
Pinch of salt
8 oz (225 g) caster sugar
Vanilla essence

1/2 pt (250 ml) whipping cream
1 tablespoon Kirsch
8 oz (225 g) fresh strawberries, washed and dried

To make the meringue, beat the egg whites together with the salt until quite stiff. Sieve in half the sugar and beat until very thick. Fold in the rest of the sugar and a few drops of vanilla essence.

Spoon into an icing bag to which a medium-sized round nozzle has been fitted. Pipe nests onto a greased baking sheet, starting from the centre and working out like a whirlpool. The firmer and steadier you can squeeze the bag, the more professional your nests will look! Bake in a very slow oven (250°F, 130°C; Gas Mark 1/2) for two or three hours until quite dry.

Whip the cream, fold in the Kirsch and pile into the nests. Arrange the strawberries halved, or quartered if they are large ones, like eggs in the nest. Chill in the coldest part of the refrigerator until required.

Arrange on a pretty plate covered with a doily (or a washed and dried fern leaf if you are really feeling artistic). Place a sheet of greaseproof paper on top of the strawberries and cover *very* lightly with clingfilm. Keep them as cool as possible.

The Party Cheescake *(serves 10–12)*

8 oz (225 g) digestive biscuits
3 oz (75 g) butter
2 oz (50 g) sugar
1/2 teaspoon cinnamon
9 oz (250 g) cream cheese
2 egg, separated
1/2 pt (250 ml) sour cream
4 oz (125 g) caster sugar

Grated rind of 1/2 lemon
1/2 teaspoon lemon juice
1/2 teaspoon vanilla essence
1 oz (25 g) plain flour
Icing sugar or 1/4 pt (150 ml) whipped cream, slices of fresh fruit and 2 oz (50 g) chopped nuts for decoration

Crush the digestive biscuits with a rolling pin. Melt the butter and sugar in a saucepan over a gentle heat. Stir in the biscuit crumbs and cinnamon and mix well. Press the mixture evenly over the bottom of a greased loose-bottomed 9–10 in (23–25 cm) round cake tin. Chill in the refrigerator.

Soften the cream cheese by beating it in a large mixing bowl. Beat in the egg yolks, sour cream, sugar, lemon juice and vanilla essence. Sift in the flour and mix thoroughly. Whisk the egg whites until stiff and fold lightly into the cheese mixture. Spoon onto the biscuit base and bake in a moderate oven (350°F, 180°C; Gas Mark 4) for about 1¼ hours or until firm to the touch. Cool the cheesecake slowly by leaving it in the switched-off oven with the door open for about 1 hour longer.

If portage of the picnic presents a problem simply douse the cheesecake with sifted icing sugar and leave it at that; if not, smother the top and/or sides with whipped cream and decorate with fruit and chopped nuts.

Red Fruit Salad Bowl *(serves 10–12)*

4 oz (125 g) caster sugar	4 oz (125 g) redcurrants
1 pt (500 ml) water	4 oz (125 g) blackcurrants
4 tablespoons blackcurrant or	8 oz (225 g) raspberries
rose-hip syrup	8 oz (225 g) strawberries, sliced
Juice of 1 orange	8 oz (225 g) red cherries, halved
Cherry brandy	and stoned

Dissolve sugar in the water over a low heat. Add syrup and bring to the boil. Simmer gently for 5 minutes. Remove from the heat and add orange juice and cherry brandy to taste.

Add the prepared red- and blackcurrants; leave aside until the syrup cools. Place remaining fruit in a large, clear plastic or glass serving bowl. Pour in the cool syrup and fruit; cover with clingfilm and leave for at least 1 hour in the refrigerator before packing carefully into an ice box.

Brandy Snaps with Whipped Cream *(makes 25–30 biscuits)*

4 oz (125 g) butter	1 teaspoon ground ginger
4 oz (125 g) soft brown sugar	1 teaspoon brandy
4 tablespoons golden syrup	Finely grated rind of 1 lemon
4 oz (125 g) plain flour	½ pt (250 ml) whipping cream

Melt the butter over a low heat; add the sugar and syrup. Stir until thoroughly blended and the sugar has dissolved. Remove from heat.

Sift the flour and ginger into the mixture; add the brandy and lemon rind, and mix thoroughly with a wooden spoon.

Set the mixture aside for a minute or two to cool down. Meanwhile apply *plenty* of grease to a few baking sheets and the handles of some wooden spoons.

Put teaspoonfuls of mixture at least 4 in (10 cm) apart on the trays and bake in a moderate oven (350°F, 180°C; Gas Mark 4) for 8–10 minutes. Remove the top tray first, allow to cool for a few seconds, then swiftly remove the biscuits with a palette knife and roll round the greased spoon handles. Repeat with the remaining trays as soon as you have finished the first. (If the biscuits harden before they have all been rolled return to the oven for a minute or two and they will become malleable again. Use the wooden spoons in rotation so that the biscuits can be left to cool on the handles for a minute or so.)

Allow to cool completely before filling with whipped cream and packing into a rigid container. If the container is both pretty and practical it can do service on the picnic table.

Hungerford Park *(serves 10–12)*

1 lemon	½ bottle Amontillado (medium)
1 orange	sherry
2 oz (50 g) caster sugar	2 large tins of light ale
2 red-skinned eating apples	Grated nutmeg
1 pt (500 ml) dry ginger ale	1 bottle dry sparkling wine

Pare the rind from the lemon and orange and squeeze the juice. Dissolve the sugar in the juice by heating gently in a saucepan. Pour over the rind and leave to cool.

Core and slice the apples and place in a large bowl. Pour over the drained, cooled syrup; add the dry ginger ale, sherry, light ale and a pinch or two of nutmeg. Mix well and leave in the refrigerator for a few hours. At the same time chill the bottle of sparkling wine.

Just before leaving, transfer punch to pre-chilled thermos flasks, including as much of the apple as possible. Take chilled wine separately and keep both cool in an ice box. For each serving pour punch ⅔ of the way up a tall glass, top with sparkling wine and mix with a long spoon or cocktail mixer.

Mulled Wine *(serves 8–10)*

1 lemon	1 dessertspoon cinnamon
1 tablespoon cloves	1 teaspoon nutmeg
3 tablespoons brown sugar	3½ pt (2 l) red wine

Pare the lemon and squeeze the juice. Put both in a large saucepan or preserving pan, and add remaining ingredients. Heat gently until *almost* boiling. Add more sugar if you like a sweeter drink. Strain into a couple of large thermos flasks and serve at the end of your *fête champêtre,* just as the chill night air begins to conquer the spirits.

INDEX

95